# THINKING
# PASSOVER

# THINKING PASSOVER

*A Rabbi's Book of*
*Holiday Values*

## Ben Kamin

A DUTTON BOOK

DUTTON
Published by the Penguin Group
Penguin Books USA Inc., 375 Hudson Street,
New York, New York 10014, U.S.A.
Penguin Books Ltd, 27 Wrights Lane, London W8 5TZ, England
Penguin Books Australia Ltd, Ringwood, Victoria, Australia
Penguin Books Canada Ltd, 10 Alcorn Avenue,
Toronto, Ontario, Canada M4V 3B2
Penguin Books (N.Z.) Ltd, 182–190 Wairau Road,
Auckland 10, New Zealand

Penguin Books Ltd, Registered Offices:
Harmondsworth, Middlesex, England

First published by Dutton, an imprint of Dutton Signet,
a division of Penguin Books USA Inc. Distributed in Canada by
McClelland & Stewart Inc.

First Printing, March, 1997
10  9  8  7  6  5  4  3  2  1

REGISTERED TRADEMARK—MARCA REGISTRADA

LIBRARY OF CONGRESS CATALOGING IN PUBLICATION DATA:
Kamin, Ben.
Thinking Passover : a rabbi's book of holiday values / Ben Kamin.
p.      cm.
Includes bibliographical references.
ISBN 0-525-94131-2
1. Passover.   2. Seder.   3. Ethics, Jewish.   I. Title.
BM695.P3K26   1997                                             96-41987
296.4'37—dc20                                                      CIP

Printed in the United States of America
Set in Weiss

*For my parents, who set the table;*
*And my parents-in-law, who added something sweet.*

# CONTENTS

# ACKNOWLEDGMENTS

As with my previous books, the words herein result from my work as a rabbi. I continue to appreciate my congregants at The Temple-Tifereth Israel in Cleveland, whose lives and prayers are so often revealed to me.

I particularly wish to acknowledge the help and insights I received while preparing this book from my colleagues at The Temple, Rabbi Rosette Barron Haim and Rabbi Dr. Roger C. Klein. Both were as generous to me with interesting texts and useful ideas as they are supportive and kind in our good and shared rabbinate.

Once again Susan Belman spent time advising me on style, structure, and relevance. I am lucky for the gifts of her wisdom and firm criticism.

My life is blessed with the presence of two publishing professionals who give substance to my dreams: Deb Brody, my editor at Dutton, and Faith Hamlin, my literary agent.

In the matter of Passover as a contemporary ideal, I am

also blessed, as are so many millions in America, with the inspiring memory of Dr. Martin Luther King, Jr. His words and vision fill these pages; freedom is an old yearning.

I thank God that my wife, Cathy, and my two sweet daughters, Sari and Debra, exchange air and values with me in the same simple house on Traver Road.

# Even God Likes a Good Story

Some people are reluctant to use garlic cloves during Passover because they believe that the garlic might have been harvested with knives that had previously been in contact with leaven. As many people know, the use of unleavened bread, matzoh, is a keynote of the holiday. There are so many things—emotional and practical—going on during the Passover season, yet some folks find themselves fretting about the ramifications of a brush with garlic.

This is exactly why I find the holiday so fascinating. Different people have different associations, different myths, and different obsessions that they bring to this remarkable and eclectic season. If it's not garlic, it might be the kind of parsley one uses. A fuss is made about plates and cutlery. Everybody has peculiar notions, even though the overriding message and urgency of the holiday remain at the center of the activities, the preparations, the emotions. Being Jews, we agree to bring a cacophony of habits to the holiday, even while listening to the symphony of meaning that Passover ultimately brings to the human family.

But in the end it's really not about garlic, parsley, silverware, or wine cups. It's not even about the matzoh or the shimmering pieces of gefilte fish bathing in white gelatin and red horseradish. It's about people, and feelings and laughter and tears. It's about remembering what your house used to smell like at this time of year, what certain people looked like and how they sounded and felt, and how that resonated through and around you. As Elie Wiesel, the twentieth-century poet of the Jewish people, has asked: "What significance does Passover have, if not to keep our memories alive?"

If Passover is about anything, it's about people remembering that something important happened long ago and also remembering to cherish the meaning of what happened. Such a relationship to the past—and to the people who inhabited the past—creates tolerance, rectitude, and maybe even love.

Passover has a way of drawing people together. It rouses us to tell, chant, or sing a famous story and therefore to ensure that we in the human family grow more familiar with one another.

The Passover story, ageless, wonderful, edifying, got its spark because of the rather mundane, agricultural reality that there was a famine in Palestine some thirty-seven centuries ago. Jacob and his sons were hungry; the resulting migration to Egypt triggered a mighty cultural confrontation that has yielded the mnemonic magic of the Passover oracles. The richness we feel in our hearts on the night of the Seder, as a grandparent or a parent ceremoniously delivers the story, all started because of a previous emptiness in somebody's belly.

I remember the power of the story on Passover night in my own home. My father, who was the storyteller, was actually a mechanical engineer who designed safety eyeware and even had a hand in the Gemini space program. But I don't remember too much about what he told me concerning hydrogen or the impact of heat on a space capsule. I do remember the stories of his wartime experiences in the newly created state of Israel, and I do recall long talks with him at the ballpark in the years just after our family immigrated to the United States. I remember listening to him, and to my mother, from my bedroom upstairs, the night they and a few of their friends sat up until dawn and talked about their old countries until the television finally announced the election of John F. Kennedy to the presidency. And I certainly remember my father conducting the Passover seder year after year in our elaborately set and converted living room. I can still hear his heavily accented pronunciation of the Ten Plagues and his deep singing of the "Dayenu" song, especially now, when it is my turn in the family history to lead my children in the ritual. The story itself connects me to that vanished living room, giving me some kind of emotional track upon which to steady my grief for my departed father and to track my wonderment at how quickly I became the father in somebody else's eyes.

My father was a scientist, and he knew a lot of facts. But the stories are what I remember.

People are the products of biology, and we were certainly created in nature. Whether one believes Darwin or the book of Genesis (or even a synthesis of the two), the fact is that human beings are flesh, blood, cells, and water. That is our organic basis. But what connects us are the circumstances of our existence, our family lines and cultural situations. Language and lore and history bind us or separate us. Stories about ourselves humanize our existence, and are used, at best, to promote and exalt ourselves or, at worst, to revile and destroy one another. Stories are indoctrinating tools that shape, bend, or thwart human life.

In recognizing the power of stories, and their potential virtue, one has to concede that they are sometimes used to condemn a group of people or an individual. In other words, there is politics in some prose, and there is even perversion in some poetry. When we assert that stories connect human souls, we must also recognize that there is a dark side to all of this. Stories that are pernicious, humiliating, even brutal continue to have an effect on how people act toward one another. The twentieth century, with its world wars, holocausts, and nuclear blasts, has been a combined story often driven by lies and vicious, stubborn myths. In the context of this book, and of our definition of Passover itself, we need to agree that the kind of stories we are talking about are those that offer a moral lesson in favor of humanity, in service to honest memory.

Stories are not always completely true, but they must always be morally genuine. It is my intent in this book to prove that the significance of Passover is in its honest commitment to human memory, to the dignity of life, and to the understandable and tender need of people to share noble traditions of families and nations.

In the beginning and in the end, human lives yield stories, accounts, anecdotes, remembrances. From birth announcements to eulogies, we are speaking and writing the diaries of our existence. If God had stopped with the water and the sky, he would have never really known about the moral inclination of his creations. Grasses do not betray feelings; human souls do. The tensions of good and evil, the interacting dramas of living and breathing entities—these are, according to Jewish tradition, what made the original creation worthwhile and interesting. God could have left well enough alone, sitting back in heaven and admiring the mountains. His business wasn't finished, however, until he dotted the valleys with people—and our day-to-day triumphs and tragedies.

After all, what is truly human about us? The answers become clear as a group of people, many from the same family, gather around a table to eat, sing, and revisit a story. On one hand, there is the old Egyptian legend being retold, and the mounting saga of freedom being relearned. On a secondary level, however, there is the more intimate, clarifying drama of the people at that table revisiting one another as relatives, friends, and neighbors. This is a story in itself—the far more psychologically redeeming recital of personal connection and self-validation. There is no question, according to Jewish tradition, that God wants to hear us retell the Egyptian story. But there can be no question either that God wants us to hear ourselves talking with one another.

Passover is a table set for meaningful tears. Some people plan for it by making a fuss over the impropriety of garlic or the permissibility of saccharin as an artificial sweetener during the festival. Indeed, certain pills and medications have to be curtailed because of the dietary restrictions of Passover. But most people, while happy to acquiesce to some form of the ritual around the Seder table, nevertheless prepare for and experience the holiday by thinking about the people, living and departed, who have made them laugh or cry during the course of this life. While readying either to tell or hear the freedom story of Moses and Pharaoh, we revisit our family story of Mom and Dad.

Judaism has a strong tradition that two concurrent bodies of law inform our lives. The Written Law, basically represented by the Torah, is traditionally associated with the revelation at Mt. Sinai. The Written Law is derived from the original Ten Commandments, which some believe were actually carved into two tablets of stone and then handed over to Moses. The rest of the Torah was written by Moses and a few other scribes, evolving into the divine scripture. The information, the meaning, and the direction are all written down for us as an eternal doctrine.

But Judaism also maintains that Moses "received" a second revelation atop Mt. Sinai. This one was not written down. It was an unscripted, continuous tradition known as the Oral Law. Moses more likely felt it than heard it or garnered it via a divine memo. The Oral Law was and is an evolving collection of opinions, discussions, instructions, fables, allegories, and aphorisms that supplement and elucidate the written law known as Torah. The Oral Law, to a great extent, is expressed in Talmudic tractates but is considered to be gloriously unfinished. It is an unbridled amalgam of traditions and insights and verses that interpret and explain human life. It is basically as holy as the written scripture, and, in a large sense, we are all its voices. The Oral Law is the absolute partner of the Written Law, flowing water to the Torah's frozen riverbed. In other words, at Mt. Sinai, Moses got both the book and the story.

There is a written and an oral experience at Passover that parallels this historic pattern. There is the text of the Haggadah, sacrosanct, vivid, timeless. But there is also the text of the human heart, alive, vital, timely. Passover asserts the holiness of both. It listens to what you say to your sister, your son, your mother. It listens as well to what you remember about your grandmother or your great-uncle. Passover sighs with relief when the telling of the Story liberates you to tell *your* story.

## Chapter One

# Unleavened Love

There are times when a table becomes the set denominator among a group of people. There are moments when a table, covered in cloth, glistening with glass and china, shining with memories, becomes a plane of goodwill. There are times when the distance between two people, seemingly so far, becomes as near as the tureen of warm chicken soup.

Such a time is Passover. Born in a national story of liberation, the holiday is renewed every year in acts of private liberation among people. At Passover, our noses tickled by sizzling spices, our eyes warmed by fragrant steams, our stomachs and hearts filled with benevolence, we find ourselves drawing from once dry wells of affection. We are able to forgive hurt feelings, and we are overcome by the sweet effects of returning home. Even if the Seder is held at a place that was not our childhood home, the fact that our living parents and grandparents are present and in charge draws us back to the more benign time when these loved ones were nigh perfect in our very needful eyes.

Think about it. We're not always sure about what our parents have done for us. We're sometimes judgmental about them, as they certainly are about us. From the time of the Bible to the time of your family and mine, parents and children have pulled at each other, sometimes helping each other, sometimes hurting one another. Families are people intertwined; sometimes we give one another a smooth piece of cord, and other times we twist it into knots.

But family love is complicated, and it usually benefits from acts of renewal. Direct moments between a father and a son, or a mother and a daughter, or a brother and a sister, are always potentially meaningful. It doesn't have to be Passover night for people either to reconcile an old difference or simply recommit to love. The trouble is that such moments of healing between people are rare; they are easily put off in a society filled with diversions, distractions, and substitute relationships.

So often adult children live hundreds if not thousands of miles from their siblings and parents. We make new friends in our new worlds who often become like family. We confide in them, we help them consecrate their children, we console them. In today's commuter culture, chances are that your soul mate at work, next door, or on the train knows more about what you feel than your sister or your father back home. This, to some degree, is a natural outgrowth of the way we live in the closing years of the twentieth century.

But then Passover comes along, with its recurring story of an entire ethnic group being whisked from slavery to freedom all together. Suddenly your grandfather at the Seder table becomes the tribal chieftain, calling you back to your original responsibilities and your fading heritage. The horseradish bites the back of your throat—a primal call of duty from the mother who once protected you, certainly guided you, and now generally feels that she has lost control over you. This is not a loosely structured discussion between family members that was planned during a sports outing or occasioned by a family milestone. There is not the forced awkwardness of a "much needed" talk. The Passover table, ordained by the religious calendar, convoked around the dining room *at home*, becomes the wonderfully indirect, carefully regulated ritual that places hot food and warm songs in between you and those you love, need, anguish over, or brood about. The effect of all of this is to streamline the emotions into a flow of ritual and merrymaking and remembrance that softens the heart, loosens the bile, renews the joy, and somehow rejoins the generations. Once again a people is set free, and finds a common board of values and concerns. Passover is the set cutlery of family therapy—a culinary and conciliatory nighttime passage that makes our parents into parents again while sending us back down a fairly delicious road to childhood. At Passover, love, like the matzoh, is unleavened.

"My mother and I don't agree on much of anything," a congregant of mine, of Moroccan descent, once told me. "She doesn't approve of the way I live. She doesn't like that I gave my children American names. She thinks I've forgotten our proud Sephardic roots. We don't share that much. But then, every Passover we bring everybody back home, and she makes me *babanatza*. I remember every mouthful from when I was little. My mother and I don't say too much to each other all year round. But when she serves that old rice pudding that she makes only on Passover, I eat and she smiles. Everything is okay. We even know that it will be okay the following Passover because we're communicating right then and there through that pudding of hers that only makes sense that night. I guess I'll have to face life someday without *babanatza*. And even though my mother and I just don't have much in common, I know that I'll feel very lonely someday without her smug face staring at me with the pudding in my mouth. I'll sure remember my mother best when Passover comes around—especially when somebody else tries and fails to make the rice pudding."

There may be more liturgy in a hefty bowl of *babanatza* or a plate of *matzoh brei* than in even the thick Yom Kippur prayer book. Indeed, at the High Holy Days, particularly Yom Kippur, we are charged to make peace with others. The Atonement Day devotions admonish us that the holiday is not strictly about God forgiving our sins. It is more about people forgiving one another; in that God is satisfied.

But how much genuine healing occurs in the synagogue during these Days of Awe? Surely some; many people bring a sincere attitude to the religious new year. They view it as a clean slate, a real safety valve that helps people relate to one another. But the effect is, to some degree, limited by the very circumstances of the gathering.

On Rosh Hashanah and Yom Kippur, people sit in a synagogue facing a lectern and not each other. The atmosphere is ornate, dramatic, starched. The center of gravity is the pulpit; the rabbi and his or her sermon tend to be the focus of the whole thing. Many of the prayers read and much of the music chanted are effective and even beautiful. But the prim setting and the somewhat choreographed atmosphere do not necessarily lend themselves to any emotional probing between people. Sitting in pews, parallel to one another, reading responsively with a cloaked figure up above, represent an important watershed for the Jewish calendar but not always that much for a singular Jewish soul.

Meanwhile, there is something curative around the Seder table, regardless of how elaborate or formal the meal is in any particular setting. Members of a family and friendship circle are sitting, facing one another, and passing each other plates of food and psalms of attachment. There is an intimacy here that cannot be replicated in the synagogue or anywhere else. And there is a special quality taken on by the leaders of the Seder who, quite frequently, are our parents. Not only do they take on an aura, but our tradition actually endows them with it. Tonight, regardless of all the emotional side trips we have taken as family members, the spiritual road leads directly back to the intersection where we see them giving birth to us, weaning us, nurturing us, raising us. Tonight they are not beholden for any of their flaws.

The fact is that at Passover, the leaders of the Seder, our ancestors, become royalty. This is a tradition that, if unknown to some, is *sensed* by almost all. The innate quality of reverence for the parent is first perceived at the very beginning of the ritual meal, as hands are washed. The cleansing occurs at several levels. Against a familiar china cabinet, just a few feet from a cherished set of family portraits, amidst some special dishes used only at such an occasion, there is entry into the very living room of the human soul. A pitcher and a basin of water are solemnly presented to the leader of the Seder. The ancestor dips his hands (frankly, it's rarely a woman, although it certainly can be) in the water and then dries his hands off with a towel especially presented for this inceptive moment. It's an act of creation; we children of any age feel that our parents are crowned again with the vestige of their generational dominion. This is exactly the intent of the night and exactly why we feel a rejuvenated loyalty to our parents, a forgiving and obliging tone that is either spoken in words, tasted in pudding, or expressed in suddenly welcome tears.

Elie Wiesel has written, in fact, about this opening moment of the rinsing of hands. Always the leader of the

Seder is given the basin first. We watch him perform the little ritual. We may even realize that we haven't looked at his hands like this in a very long time. "He is served first," writes Wiesel in his *A Passover Haggadah*, "because tonight he is king in his home. Leaning back on a cushion like a citizen of ancient Rome, he enjoys the privileges of sovereignty."

Now, we adult children may be very successful in life. In America many of us have been blessed with professional and material prosperity. Coming to the Seder, we momentarily leave behind our business empires, replete with secretaries, cellular phones, fax machines, voice mail, and a host of other cable and fiber-optic connections. Even those of us who are not masters of our own careers feel an understandable pride in whatever we have achieved. We usually think of ourselves as having succeeded to something better than our parents (which is exactly what they prayed would happen to us). Yes, we are important and even powerful people with a great deal of savvy and sophistication. In some cases many other people answer to us.

But when we come home to our parents on Passover and somebody passes our father or grandfather a basin of water from which to wash hands, we suddenly remember that we are but children. We were born to a mother and a father who set the table of life for us. This comes home to us as we come home to them. Their abiding royalty is as poignant for us this night as their mortality is evident, particularly as we present them with our own children—

their regal legacy. As hands are washed and blessings spoken—often under the same roof where we once frolicked with much younger parents—we are overcome with the realization that, after all, our parents are the king and queen of a private world unavailing to dictaphones, corporate cards, and company cars.

Our parents, masters of the Seder, royalty of the season, guide us even when they are no longer with us. Such is the power of this holiday that evokes memory in a far more meaningful way than the reading of a memorial list in the synagogue.

I remember going "home" to Cincinnati during a recent Passover. The festive meal was taking place in my mother's house. My mother, known for her unusual, Israeli-style *haroset* made with apples, wine, and, of all things, peanut butter, set the table with parsley, white strips of horseradish root (she believes you ought truly know from the bitter), and her memories of my father. My mother and father, both born in British Palestine, had grown up together sharing springtime Seders near the Samarian mountains of the Holy Land. When they and their classmates declared, "Next year in Jerusalem!" at the close of the meal, they were making a direct, political statement. After 1948, when Israel became an independent nation, they changed the verse to "This year in Jerusalem!"

My mother and her generation experienced their own true exodus in this century. My father was, of course, king of my childhood Seders. As a young man in 1948, he had been one of those soldiers in Israel's Haganah defense league who helped rescue refugees from Europe's displaced-persons camps. They, refugees who survived the Holocaust, arrived in rickety, leaky boats that attempted to evade the British coastal blockade of those years. The freedom drama depicted in the Passover Haggadah was something my parents had known personally and dangerously. Unlike the Red Sea epic, the waters of this sea parted only to the extent that courageous men and women were able to outsmart the British and outswim the Mediterranean.

Understandably, my father is missed when we convene for the Seder in my mother's house. On this occasion, several years after losing our dad, my brother, Sam, my sister, Tami, and I arrived with our spouses, our children, and our mixed feelings of reunion and remembrance. My brother took it upon himself to lead this particular Seder.

As the evening began, my brother passed out the old Haggadah books that we had used for so many years. There is an endless variety of these Passover manuals; we shared the venerable Maxwell House edition that is heavy on the Hebrew and light on the artwork. The books are wrinkled from many hands, marked with stains from soup, wine, coffee, and tears. Sam reached into the dining room cabinet to retrieve the books with the gravity of a curator in a private museum. He distributed them carefully, lovingly, and seemed intent on handing me one in particular.

I realized quickly that I had a distinct Haggadah, indeed. It was the one my father had used for years to lead the Seder. Sighing to myself, I recognized his handwritten commentary in the book, along the margins. In a quiet shock of recognition I observed his slanted, Semitic handwriting in the myriad fussy notes to himself. My brother wanted to lead the Seder in his own right, but he handed me the responsibility of holding the Passover-driven legacy. Our father had, over the years, jotted down an entire personal guide of data, instructions, comments, and directions that he used in conjunction with the text of Passover night.

At one point in the Seder, Sam wasn't altogether certain how to proceed. There is some flexibility in the ritual. Certain Haggadah books are more detailed than others; reasonable deviation and improvisation is permitted and acceptable. Sam looked up and indicated that he did not recall what exactly the next step would be. He glanced around the table, amiably anticipating a suggestion. I looked up from the page in my book and announced: "He tells us what to do." Then, reading from what had been inscribed neatly in the book, I declared: "Now turn to page 27 and ask the children to sing."

We in fact did turn to page 27, and my father's grandchildren were soon singing. Sam, Tami, and I sat in praise, feeling as though our collective shoulder had been tapped from heaven. It was altogether wonderful and redeeming—a personal exodus that we shared around the table. At that moment, as my mother encouraged us to make and taste the bittersweet "Hillel sandwich" that combines the horseradish with the sweet *haroset*, we realized that—if we were willing—our parents would always leave their handwriting in our lives. We are determined to do the same for our children; Passover is the natural slate. With his peculiar, slanted script, my father was still there, reclining royally at the Seder table.

My friend Linda remembers celebrating Passover in the small community of Dixon, Illinois. Her mother, Betty, was an informal spokesperson and advocate for the tiny Jewish minority in this town, best known for harvesting petunias and the early career of Ronald Reagan. "It was a very major observance," recalls Linda, now the mother of three small children. "It was the central event of our religious life. Everything happened the same way each year, and it made my siblings and me feel secure and good about who we were. There was only a small synagogue in town, and we had a lot of different rabbis. My parents brought the Judaism home to us each year through the Passover. We always had a lot of people in the house, and Dad would very solemnly conduct the proceedings. For months prior, Mom and Dad would make the preparations. There was hardly a kosher butcher in town, but somehow Mom always managed to get a shank bone. You just knew that shank bone would be there in the middle of the table. I think I know that I'm Jewish because I always knew that my mother would make the arrangements to have that shank bone delivered for our Passover table every spring. I remember Mom best doing that."

Linda also remembers her mother's activities on behalf

of the Jewish community in that small town in the heart-land. "Mom went around to all the schools in town and explained Jewish values and history. She'd show up in the school building and pull out a cardboard backing from a dry-cleaned shirt. She'd make her presentation using a marker right on that poster board. That's how she did it. She'd write out Jewish ideas, like the Ten Commandments or what the Talmud is and how it gave so many concepts to western civilization. She'd appear at civic functions and proudly give a lecture on Judaism. At home, she made us unafraid to be Jewish in a very Christian environment. But she always got that shank bone. And we'd always invite a stranger or two who was in town to our Seder, because that is the custom."

Linda told me about Passover in Dixon, Illinois, just a few months after her mother died in 1995. "I do the Passover exactly the way she did—without even thinking about it. I have her recipes, and I buy the same kinds of ingredients for everything she made in Indianapolis. Of course, I get a shank bone, although it's not as difficult for me here. But what I remember the best about Mom was the magnificent Seder plate she always put down in the middle of the table. It was grand and had a slot for each of the central foods."

Linda went on to describe her mother's Seder plate in detail. It is a blue and yellow piece of Armenian pottery that, naturally, Linda has in her home. Her own children watch her gently laying the plate down in the middle of a new generation, across a table that links mother to daughter, grandchildren to matriarch.

An Armenian platter is set down in one home, a bowl of pudding is served in another. Somebody's handwriting appears along the margins of a story book with little notes as holy to the reader as the old text itself. Beyond words, beyond formality, beyond the need to be clever or coy, we return to a world where parents and children are completely themselves. At Passover, our ancestors linger around a table as perfect once again as they were when they first told about us about creation.

*Chapter Two*

---

᭡ᩂᨀᩂᨃ

# Matzoh and Memory

Years ago, while living as a child in Israel, I had a rather boisterous great-aunt who enjoyed recounting tales of the early days of Israel's settlement. Some of my ancestors were directly involved in reclaiming the Jewish homeland; Aunt Esther was a kind of personal family historian. She would reminisce about the old personalities, recalling their exploits, their trials, their foibles. But she never discussed their arguments with one another. "After all this time," declared Esther with a twinkle in her eye, "all is forgiven and forgotten." It was sweet, I suppose, even if it was not altogether guileless.

Meanwhile, an old French press law, dating back to 1881, makes it illegal for anyone to discuss publicly any former acts of punishments or cruelty that have already been officially "forgotten" by the state. A number of well-known crimes have eventually received clemency in France, including the notorious Dreyfus Affair, pardoned in 1900. Even the collaboration of French citizens with the Nazis was partially forgiven in the early 1950s; these decrees of purposeful amnesia are ostensibly designed to re-create national unity and to encourage the nation to go forward.

It should be noted that these amnesty laws of France are ultimately paper acts. There remains a great deal of serious soul-searching and historical anguish in France among thoughtful people who ruminate about everything from the Bartholomew's Day Massacre of 1572 to the beheading of King Louis XVI during the French Revolution to the blatant anti-Semitism that indicted Captain Alfred Dreyfus in 1894.

But there is no amnesia in Passover. Nor is anyone, even living now, permitted emotional amnesty from its chronicles. One of the most remarkable sentences of the Haggadah is the one that, in one form or another, states: "In every generation, each one of us is to feel as though we personally left Egypt." In fact, the Bible actually has a verse, written in the present tense, that reads: "It is because of that which God did for me when I came out of Egypt . . ." Likewise, a more mystical tradition among the Jews suggests that all our souls were actually there at the time. One way or another, our direct, fervent involvement in the drama of slavery and freedom is mandated by Passover. There is no statute of limitations on this topic; nor is any kind of legislative act going to be enacted that might help forgive or erase the national memory.

It should also be noted that no edition of the Haggadah reads that "every Jew" must feel as though he or she had personally left Egypt. The Hebrew text clearly says "every person." This holiday, in the very way it chooses its words, has much to say about the power of memory in human life generally. Certainly, Abraham Lincoln drew some insight on the evil of slavery from the Passover story that called upon him—like anybody else—to feel personally involved in the flight to freedom. Surely no Jew among the many who participated in the American civil rights movement of the 1950s and 1960s stopped short because he or she thought that the discussion of human dignity was confined to Jewish experiences.

Passover asks people to store values in our minds even if we weren't personally present at the episode that informs our memory. The device for recollection is the matzoh found at the table. Dry, brittle, so different than the kinds of bread that we normally eat, matzoh is the flaky, flat contract between ourselves and the chronicles.

I sometimes wonder about the power of matzoh. It is a most nondescript food, an almost vapid blend of flour and water. In some ways it is the perfect culinary equivalent of Jewish history: It is fragile, connected to events much larger than any one meal, and it depends upon the sympathetic intervention of other factors (in this case, like some margarine or a good jam) to be properly enjoyed. Bite into it, and you know that you are experiencing an emotional journey somewhere. You are commanded, early in the Passover meal, to spread some horseradish on it and then to literally ingest the reality of the bitterness of slavery. Matzoh doesn't exist just for the sake of taste, even though in recent years it has gained in popularity among the health-conscious who appreciate its low-fat content.

Yet a critical moment of the Seder occurs when the leader reads the following phrase out loud, while indicating the matzoh: "This is the bread of affliction, which our ancestors ate in Egypt. Let all who are hungry come and eat. Let all who are in need come and share our meal." You have a situation here that directs a modern participant at a dining room table, coiffured and nicely dressed, to actually relate to the misery and the yearnings of ancient Hebrew slaves as though that twentieth-century participant had personally experienced the degradation of bondage. And when you, the participant, are drawn into this on that level, you actually "recall" how terrible it was to be excluded from life's goodness. This, in turn, makes your subsequent invitation to the hungry more a matter of conviction than just a perfunctory pronouncement.

The fact is that this matzoh, dry, tough-textured, long-lasting (all attributes of the Jewish people), turns your taste buds in favor of social justice. This isn't just a casual visit with Wonder Bread, and it is quite different than the meeting of some warm rye bread with a pile of juicy corned beef. But it is not only in the process of eating unleavened bread that values are digested; the very method of its preparation is meant to impart meaning and to invoke memory.

It should be noted, particularly by those who find meaning in the Bible, that there is a disproportionate

amount of attention given in the scripture to the prohibition of leaven. Given all the other, loftier issues and stories included in the biblical text, one might wonder about
the near obsession regarding leavened and unleavened
bread. There is a small narrative in Genesis—long before
Moses was even born and the Exodus drama unfolded—in
which a character named Lot receives sudden guests.
Hospitality to strangers, a key theme of the Passover
teachings, was paramount in the Middle East (it still is a
trademark of the Bedouin peoples). Not wanting his
guests to have to wait too long, Lot *"made them a feast, and
baked them unleavened bread, and they ate."*

This notion of a "hurry-up" bread, born of social circumstances, meant to impart a human value, is essentially
formalized during what the Bible solemnly calls "a night
of watching" in the Exodus story. The night of watching
was, of course, the unforgettable night when the Hebrew
slaves escaped to freedom. So, on such a night, does the
Bible tell us that the Hebrews sang songs? Did they break
out into a group dance, or call upon their leaders to write
poetry? All of these kinds of things would eventually
occur during their desert adventure, but not on that first
night of watching. That night, the Bible tells us specifically, *"they baked unleavened cakes of the dough that they brought
out of Egypt, for it was not leavened, because they were thrust out of
Egypt and could not tarry."*

An entire night of remarkable events—a landmark passage in all of human history—was convoked with a bunch

of matzoh. Over and over, in various biblical passages, the people are admonished to eat only unleavened bread in conjunction with this drama. Leavened bread became something of a taboo when it came to remembering and observing the famous freedom night. Again and again the Bible instructs us that *"seven days you shall eat unleavened bread . . . put away the leaven of your house."* There is even a warning that *"whoever eats leavened bread from the first day until the seventh day* (of Passover), *that soul shall be cut off from Israel."*

I prefer not to read that last phrase from Exodus literally, particularly since the Passover seder is designed to be so inclusive in its tone. Since so much of Jewish tradition is, in fact, allegory, my understanding of the warning about a soul being cut off from Israel is that if you don't share in the eating of unleavened bread, you won't be able to join in the memory. And if you don't remember, then, in a sense, you are cut off from the history.

But we can have no illusions about the centrality of this tension between unleavened and leavened breads that is renewed every springtime in Jewish lives. Some Jews undertake a serious search for even the most obscure crumb of leavened bread in the days before Passover. Bearing candles in the night, carrying special, ritualistic wooden spoons, they scour their shelves for any trace of leaven even as we all search our souls when this holiday approaches. More traditional Jews, absolutely diligent about the matzoh, even require a particularly regulated matzoh bread that is used only on the days of the Seder meals. This round, charred matzoh is called *matzoh she-murah*, which means "the watched matzoh." This matzoh is prepared under strict rabbinic supervision. There is a direct relationship between this distinct, opening matzoh of the festival—considered even more sacrosanct than the rest of the matzoh consumed during the holiday—and that original "night of watching." The very wheat used in this particular matzoh is guarded from the time of its harvest until the paste is prepared and the baking begins. When you taste this slightly burned, uneven matzoh, you are tasting slavery. It gives the Seder a flavor of great age. It makes you "remember." It deepens the occurrence of digestion to an experience of thought, concern, and inquiry.

A dazzling array of rabbinic rules attend to this and all the holiday matzohs, including a meticulous guide for the kneading and baking of the dough, how long it is warmed, when it is eaten, and what makes it religiously suitable. There simply can't be any fermentation in the process, even as there was no spoiling in God's commitment to protect and rescue the Hebrews on a very hurried and holy night that could allow no compromises.

In the matter of Passover, when you are trying to teach people to remember something, you even teach them how to eat the memories. Not all of us are swept away by the conscientious politics of fermentation. Nor are we all as obsessed by the religious controversies of unleavened versus leavened bread. We don't all need to be fundamentalists here; the Passover Haggadah begins and ends with inclusiveness, tolerance, compassion. But there is no question that, philosophically, matzoh bread represents a real engagement with the idea of some kind of spiritual purity in human life. There just can't be any fermentation when it comes to protecting and maintaining freedom and dignity.

For a long time now, the Jewish people have carried forward the sentiment, through the very composition of the unleavened Passover bread, that there mustn't be any corrupting elements in the dough of human civilization. This is what I "remember" when I first bit into the flat cakes every spring. This is what I relate to in the matter of the "night of watching." This is what I want my daughters to recall—not exactly how long the flour and water interacted in the baker's oven, but how long people have been interacting in my daughters' school, in our neighborhood, across our land. If there was no time for our ancestors to bake full loaves of bread, then there is no time for us today to wallow while others are hungry. If the Bible keeps hinting, even through peculiar tales and severe decrees, that you're supposed to feed guests or even needy strangers in a hurry, then I'll take that notion, along with my children, to my community halls, to my synagogue, and certainly to the nearest hunger center.

Matzoh, whether it's prepared to this specification or that, will remain only as prosaic as our lack of ideas that go with it. Eat it, and you may well recall that you were born without a wallet. Taste it, and you may realize, again, that life is fickle, short, sometimes short of the blessings you may take for granted. Swallow this flat bread, and you may swallow some of the endemic "puffiness" to which we are prone. Take in this strange, timeless bread, which the ancient Jewish philosopher Philo called "the clearest possible example of a food free from admixture . . . providing nothing save what is indispensable for its use," and you may find yourself returning to the flat plane of what were once your basic values and ideals.

Indeed, Philo, who lived in Alexandria during the time of Jesus, seemed to anticipate some of modern, suburban haughtiness when he contemplated unleavened bread, Passover, and human values. He wrote that "leaven is forbidden because of the rising which it produces." Two thousand years ago, long before the rising affluence of much of our civilization, the rabbi stated, in connection with matzoh:

> *Here again we have a symbol of the truth, that none as he approaches the altar should be uplifted or puffed up by arrogance; rather gazing on the greatness of God, let him gain a perception of the weakness which belongs to the creature, even though he may be superior to others in prosperity; and having been thus led to the reasonable conclusion, let him reduce the overweening exaltation of his pride by laying low that pestilent enemy—conceit.*

Matzoh, bland, breakable, primitive, a kind of bread of the people, reminds us that we alone can add ingredients that both enliven and corrupt human life. Eaten by itself, we think again of what is pristine in our lives. Shared with others, it reminds us that the world is only as humane as what we all bring to it. No wonder somebody important in our lives points at it at least once a year, calling it the bread of meaning. Meanwhile, it cries out to us to spread a layer of compassion across its fragile lines.

## Chapter Three

# Children and Curiosity

I t's amazing what a simple piece of parsley can accomplish. This cultivated herb, with its extensively curled leaves, would appear to be weak and retiring—a quiet, simple subject of the plant kingdom. It lacks much taste and is, frankly, not thought about very often except perhaps by those who are invested with the intricacies of cookery. I daresay it is mainly considered in a presentation of food for its green, decorative appearance. But parsley has power, and it certainly has implications in the Passover order of things.

Years ago, while training for the rabbinate, I served a "student pulpit" in the town of Portsmouth, Ohio. The sleepy, rather grimy small city included a Jewish congregation of some twenty-five families. One Passover night I enjoyed the Seder meal with others in the home of two aging sisters, Thelma and Cynthia Gommel. The spinsters, both wonderful cooks and kind human beings, had prepared a holiday meal of exceptional quality and grace.

There was Israeli wine that the sisters had imported from Cincinnati, stuffed gefilte fish they brought in from Columbus, hard-boiled eggs in saltwater, sizzling soup with *kneidlach* acquired in Huntington, West Virginia, turkey with matzoh dressing, honeyed sweet potatoes, and a green salad. The evening would finish with assorted nuts, sponge cake, fresh fruit, macaroons, and coffee ground from beans that had been mailed by a cousin in Fort Lauderdale.

I noticed from the start that there were many layers of parsley leaves garnishing the plates. The sisters grew the plants in their own backyard garden, in the Scioto hills. There, along the Ohio River, at the confluence of Ohio and West Virginia, we sang songs of freedom, we recounted the plagues, and we rejoiced in the liberation of the Hebrew slaves. The freedom story of Israel is surely portable. But meanwhile the preponderance of parsley struck my interest.

"It's wonderful for the digestion," said Thelma with a satisfied smile. Her hair in a tight bun, her face wrinkled with age and sweetness, she offered me yet another healthy petal of the herb as the meal ended. Cynthia nodded with encouragement. "We've had a lot of spicy foods," said the latter sister. "Chew on some parsley. It will instantly clear your tongue and freshen your taste." Indeed, the parsley refreshed my palate in a peaceable way, without the intrusiveness of drugstore mints that disinfect the mouth and sterilize the effects of a meal worth remembering along the linings of one's mouth.

The parsley, green, gentle, a bit wild, certainly had captured my regard that evening in Portsmouth. It helped transform the night. And indeed, that is a key function of this wily leaf—to arouse the curiosity, to engage the involvement of people, especially children on a long night of textual and emotional exploration.

At the outset of the Seder, a firm custom known as "karpas" takes place. It involves some greens, normally parsley, a bowl of saltwater, and one's hands. Nobody has eaten anything yet; essentially only the candle lighting, the blessing over the wine, and the washing of hands have taken place. The fact is that the children at the table—for whom the entire evening is dedicated—have already sat through a short litany of rituals. Judaism, dripping with practicality, doesn't want to lose these young minds before the evening has even unfolded. So now here comes a collection of these leafy green vegetables— bright, strange, hinting at spring. The parsley is dipped into the saltwater. A blessing is solemnly said, thanking God for creating "the fruit of the earth." The unusual combination of parsley and saltwater is then eaten. According to the tradition, this is done "to whet the appetite." But it's more than the appetite that is being teased here. The idea, plain and simple, is to get the kids to react and say to themselves, or out loud: "What's this all about? Why the green things? Why saltwater?" The reality is that the parsley is presented to arouse the curiosity of the children as the long evening begins. A child who is curious is a child who will learn.

Now, the pitch for the youngsters' involvement notwithstanding, both the parsley and the saltwater do represent certain things. As suggested, the green leaves remind the participant that spring—a time of expectation and renewal—is the season that Passover heralds. The earth is ripening, buds are maturing, there are new ideas in the warming wind. Even as the cold grip of slavery was finally loosening from the Hebrew slaves, so are the waters of hope recovering from the hard freeze of winter. Judaism has never lost its association with the cycles of nature; though it is now primarily an urban sect, the Hebrew religion took hold firmly in the soils and skies of ancient Israel.

We were originally an agricultural people who made pilgrimages to the Temple Mount in conjunction with the harvest periods of the land. Our calendar was and is the manuscript of the moons. In our prayers, we did and still do thank God every morning for the rising and setting of the sun. We started eating green herbs at Passovers ranging back to the times of the Talmud. The fact is that there is a direct, tender connection between Thelma and Cynthia Gommel's parsley garden in Portsmouth, Ohio, and the flowering hills of Jerusalem.

But in a parlor in Long Island, a dining room in San Francisco, or a synagogue social hall in Toronto, a burst of parsley can surely raise the eyebrows of little children and possibly their attention span. Then we take that parsley—and the children's interest—and dip it all into a small pool of tears. The saltwater, glistening in a bowl, strangely familiar in taste, is the teacher of life's prevailing lesson: People who are enslaved are people who weep, even in the threshold of springtime. Passover is a time for children to learn, even if the learning comes from combining unlikely foods into a hands-on lesson plan.

One of the fondest memories we have about our childhood seders is the drama of the *afikoman*. This occurs immediately following the presentation of the parsley; the youngsters have been engaged by the burst of green vegetable, and we adults plunge full force in maintaining their interest. What happens is that the head of the table takes the middle matzoh and ceremoniously breaks it in half. The larger of the two pieces is wrapped in a large napkin and becomes the mysterious *afikoman*. The children are keenly focused on this small theater because this special, broken bit of bread will be somehow whisked away and hidden from sight. The children know that they will be asked to find it near the end of the festive meal and the finder will gain a prize. Most households, of course, offer consolation prizes to all of the children who take part in "the search" with the winner earning something special.

But it's not just a game, this *afikoman* routine. The word comes from the original Greek, *epikomion*, meaning after-dinner festivities. There are a couple of serious ideas meant to be taught by this little exercise—beyond its very pragmatic implications for the children.

The larger piece of matzoh, wrapped and exalted for later discovery, is meant to teach us about the reality of hunger in our world. The simple act of breaking off the *afikoman* in the midst of a full table has deep connotations. At a moment like that, we adults and children can surely identify with the millions of people in every corner of the earth who, in fact, must salvage and set aside small bits of bread in order to survive. Many people are afraid to eat their bread and must always leave something for later on. Many American Jews, blessed with prosperity, lose sight of the reality of the ghettos—our own across the centuries as well as the ghettos of this land that afflict families who live just minutes from our own warm and sated homes. Jewish children had to horde broken pieces of bread in places like Lodz and Warsaw and Odessa not so many years ago. Many of them died for the lack of a slice of matzoh or anything else; they could have hardly imagined the luxury of the accompanying napkin. Children of all kinds suffer similarly right this minute in places such as Memphis, Cleveland, the Bronx, Savannah, East St. Louis, Fort Worth, Denver, and Los Angeles. As far as what Judaism wants to teach somebody—even in the tiny matter of setting aside a simple piece of flat bread—there is a straight line drawn from the hunger of the Hebrews in ancient Egypt to that of anybody in America.

So we get the attention of the children with transactions involving parsley, saltwater, and hidden matzoh, but we are trying to set the stage for some learning as well. There is plenty to be said, as a Seder begins, about the meaning of the season, the function of human tears, the implications of food. As far as the *afikoman* is concerned, it is hidden and it will be redeemed at the end of the evening by a child curious and lucky enough to learn that the future is not guaranteed unless we take the time to set aside some care, some hope, some consideration, and certainly some bread.

Incidentally, some mystical Jews contend that the hiding of the special matzoh and its revelation later foreshadows the future coming of a messiah. I prefer to teach, however, that the future depends upon us, and not on some intervention from the heavens. If God steps in to release people from trouble, from poverty, and from inequity, that will be fine. But meanwhile, until God arrives, we're better off teaching our children to take some responsibility for the civilization they will inherit.

If anyone has a quarrel with what I'm asserting, I encourage that person to read the Bible. All one has to do is to read from the farewell sermon given by Moses, and recorded in the closing sections of the Book of Deuteronomy. It is here that the old teacher summarizes the possibilities for divine intervention in human situations. In his talk, he actually *downplays* the role of messianic or apocalyptic safety valves:

> *The teaching I enjoin upon you this day is not too baffling for you, nor is it beyond your reach. It is not in the heavens, that you should say, "Who among us can go up to the heavens and get it for us and impart it to us, that we may observe it?" Neither is it beyond the sea, that you should say, "Who among us can cross to the other side of the sea and get it for us and*

*impart it to us, that we may observe it?" No, the thing is very
close to you, in your mouth and in your heart, to observe it.*

It's pretty clear to me that the Jewish tradition ex-
pects us to take responsibility for making things happen.
Miracles are certainly appreciated in our tradition, but the
finest miracle occurs when a child learns something.

The place of education in Jewish life has to be understood. It resides in first place. The Hebrew experience in
the desert began with ideas. The slaves were transformed
into free people via laws, concepts, aphorisms. They
learned from large-scale experiences. The Egyptians endured plagues; the Hebrews themselves were liberated
only after a drawn-out, processed, ideological confrontation between Moses and Pharaoh in a public courtyard.
The Hebrews crossed a parted sea, and then received the
foundation principles of the Ten Commandments in a
spectacular, nocturnal display of lightning and smoke.
The entire notion of freedom was written out in an elaborate contract meant not just to get those people out, but
to get them *into* a wholly new ideology of commitment,
community, and eventual literacy. If we parents wish to
get our children's attention with a bit of parsley, God got
the attention of the children of Israel with a whole lot of
fire. In both cases somebody was supposed to appreciate a
new way of looking at things.

We started with learning—even before we got our
inherited strip of land along the Mediterranean. When we
were dispossessed of our commonwealth in Judea, we

maintained Judaism by writing and studying the Talmudic literature, including a tractate about how to observe the Passover. Whenever we were exiled, from Spain, from England, from Russia, we left carrying our Torah scrolls. Wherever we arrived, in Holland, in Morocco, in America, we first built a school. The school came before the synagogue, or they were combined into one institution. Why are the Jews still here, even after the Nazi insanity of the twentieth century? The answer has much to do with our inveterate feeling for the sanctity of education. When children stop learning, a nation stops breathing.

Indeed, history tells us that when the Germans overran Poland in 1939, they immediately closed down the Jewish schools. One has to understand that the Jewish community of Poland, with its many great centers, its synagogues, cultural centers, its indomitable literature, and over three million co-religionists, had been—in spite of centuries of repression and pogroms—the world hub of Jewish life and lore. Virtually all of Poland's three million Jews were annihilated by the Nazi genocide; this represented half of the Jewish victims of the Holocaust. But the fact is that before they started killing Jewish adults and children, the Germans systematically shut down Jewish schoolhouses. The Germans, of course, then proceeded to requisition all the property associated with these buildings.

This sinister process was documented by the late Lucy Dawidowicz in her landmark work, *The War Against the Jews*. But Dawidowicz also pointed to something else.

"The Germans," she noted, "intended to deprive Jewish children of education, but they underestimated the place of education in the system of Jewish values." From parsley to parchment, the Jews are inexorably devoted to the processes of teaching, thinking, and learning.

Some remarkable things happened among the Jews during the Holocaust—from the setting of secret Sabbath tablecloths in the "paradise camp" of Theresienstadt to the holding of underground Passover seders in the Warsaw ghetto. The yearning for religious and general literacy did not die with the Jewish people—even when the whole people was necessarily hidden as a kind of national *afikoman*. It is almost uncanny, but we know that in Poland clandestine schools came into being even as the mechanism of mass murder went into full force. The Jewish people answered cruelty with ideas.

In Warsaw, site of the infamous ghetto, hundreds of small, informal classes of about ten children—each group called a *komplet*—popped up in back kitchens, in hidden attics, behind homes. In places such as Kovno, Vilna, Lublin, Lodz, and Krakow, Jewish children studied secretly in covert *hedarim* (youth academies) and illicit Talmud-Torah schools. There wasn't necessarily any collusion among the secret schools from the various communities, just as Jews in diverse places don't necessarily check with each other on the disposition of Seder gatherings on Passover. Some things just happen; they are dictated by the calendar, by tradition, or, in Poland during the Holocaust, by the ingrained Jewish instinct that knowledge is life.

In good times, the awareness of children can be aroused by the appearance of parsley; in bad, by the possibility of blood. The secret Jewish pupils of World War II became experienced in their bittersweet enterprise. When, during the course of a session, word suddenly arrived that the Germans were coming, the children would react with discipline and cleverness, transforming a classroom back into a shoemaker's shop, or quickly hiding books between trousers and stomachs, inside jackets or coats.

It was this desperate dynamic of learning that helped give life some meaning at a time when life lacked hope. Professor Dawidowicz has written: "Like bread and potatoes, education and culture sustained life in the ghetto." The parsley of existence certainly lost its verdant quality for the tragic Jews of that time and place, but it did garnish their situation to some limited degree.

The secret schools, besides imparting education to disenfranchised and accursed children, gave the communities a measure of love, physical warmth, and emotional security at a time of unyielding harshness and ugliness. The Jews, dealing with tremendous boredom as well as the danger, were inspired by the little academies. They formed card-playing societies, theater guilds, music circles, and symphony orchestras.

The presence of the furtive classes helped to create other circumstances. Strangers took to consoling one another, sharing books, engaging in stimulating debate, developing archives for each other's dairies, sheet music, artwork, and photographs. In many places, significant libraries were formed, replete with primitive but real circulation catalogs, borrowing cards, and membership rosters. It turns out that small acts of civilization helped to soothe the unceasing ache of our national predicament. Certainly the Jews—like so many other tortured groups of people under the Nazis—found resourcefulness, will, and a measure of humanity in the quiet responses of teaching and learning. So every time we summon a child's curiosity via a parsley leaf or a piece of designated matzoh, we save a mind and thereby save the world. And every time we wrap that *afikoman* in a napkin, hiding it away, we invoke the memory of so many instances in human life when people had to either learn, love, or even eat in secret. Meanwhile, for the Jewish people, wisdom is vitality, knowledge is holiness, education is life.

Indeed, it was long before the physical trials of the Holocaust and the more benign but real spiritual trials of our own affluent era that the sanctity of our children was established for the Jewish people. Even Pharaoh in Egypt knew what the Germans in Poland understood—that to shut down the Jews, you must shut down the children.

It turns out that before the actual Exodus from Egypt, there was almost an earlier escape by the Hebrews. Moses and Aaron had paid several visits to Pharaoh's court, each time repeating God's demand to "let my people go." On one occasion it seemed as though the king was going to give in to the moral outrage of the Hebrew spokesmen.

To paraphrase the discourse in the Book of Exodus, Moses at one point tells Pharaoh that the Hebrews want some time to go out into the desert and offer "a feast unto the Lord." The Hebrew leader, frankly, was going to use this supposed festival as a cover for an early exit with his people. He indicated to a skeptical but attentive Pharaoh that the slaves needed the emotional release of a community festival. He appealed to the sensibilities of the king that the people needed a religious convocation in order to deal with the hardship of their situation.

Had Pharaoh completely agreed to this proposal, the great exodus from Egypt would have taken place without the eventual cataclysm of the Ten Plagues. The climactic traumas, involving the eventual deaths of Egypt's firstborn sons, the dramatic departure after the flyover of the Angel of Death, the pursuit to the Red Sea, and the eventual mass drowning of the Egyptians might have been avoided. One could agree, however, that we who revisit the story every Passover would have less to learn as well.

But Pharaoh was as sly as he was obdurate. Responding to Moses' request for a spiritual pilgrimage to the countryside, he said: "You can go and do that. You can go, and you can take along your cattle. But not so your children."

This ugly rejoinder, that any people would possibly consider going forward without its children, is as revealing as it is cynical. Pharaoh understood history well when he made Moses this offer that, of course, had to be refused. Without the children, whose curiosity would be piqued by the sparkling little leaf of parsley? For whom would the delicious mystery of the *afikoman* be displayed and taught? At the Seder table, little ones arrive, hungry and restless. We are the ones telling the story, even as we are the ones protecting them, growing them, nourishing them. At the Seder table, the past and the future laid out before us, we realize that our responsibility to children is to feed their souls even as we fill their bellies.

## Chapter Four

# What's the Point After the Holocaust?

It may seem strange, but I have always been a bit obsessed with the date of April 19, 1943. My feeling for this generally inconspicuous date in world history has to do with a combination of things: a love of the religious calendar, a respect for history, and a deeply personal identification with the national, often anguished story of the Jewish people.

Most people who know anything about this troubled century would look upon the date of April 19, 1943, and recognize it as a day in the midst of World War II. Indeed, the war was far from over at that point; Germany still had a great deal of force and manpower and still had a great many Jews to kill. The Allies had not yet launched their much anticipated invasion of the continent. That would not take place until D-Day, June 6, 1944—when a massive force stormed heavily fortified French beaches, including Normandy. The fact is, that on April 19, 1943, although a struggling England and her allies still valiantly stayed the Nazi onslaught, America was still regrouping from the Pearl Harbor debacle, and, generally, victory was hardly in sight for the Allies.

So why the focus on April 19, 1943? It just happened to be the first night of Passover in that horrifying year— when the very thrust of the liberation story was so cruelly mocked and nullified by acts of brutality and genocide beyond human comprehension. In Warsaw, the trapped Jews of the notorious ghetto were observing both the besieged holiday and the beginnings of their courageous revolt against the German occupiers. Their situation was completely desperate, even as their Seder tables were empty. The irony of the predicament was not lost on them. For some the presence of the Passover holiday offered a little bit of inspiration, even hopefulness. For most it just added to the bitterness, the grief, and the helplessness.

In Warsaw, on the night of April 19, 1943, Passover was received by the doomed Jews of the ghetto with an uncommon mixture of emotions. The wine was watery, matzoh was scarce, and the Angel of Death was categorically *not* passing over the homes of the Hebrews. The children were asking questions, as they are charged to do on the night of Seder. But these were not the usual questions posed by our tradition.

In his account, "The Last Passover in the Warsaw Ghetto," Wladyslaw Pawlak created characters based upon real people who were in Warsaw during that fateful and final Passover. The youngest person present, as has always been the tradition at the Seder, rose to ask the Four Questions, but then changed them to fit the grievousness of the situation. For example, the child modified the question about why we eat only unleavened bread on Passover night: "And why do we have neither leavened nor unleavened bread this night?" Pawlak writes:

> As they proceeded, their voices became more and more vengeful, and they spoke the words in anger. No one was thinking of the ancient past in the valley of the Nile. The oppressor they faced was a hundredfold worse. He was alive and powerful, and only a few walls and the dusk of spring night separated him from them.

According to this account, recounted in Philip Goodman's *The Passover Anthology*, a youngster cried out about the whole ceremony: "It's a lie!" In fear and fury he protested: "God has never freed us from bondage. . . . We were slaves by the rivers of Babylon; Spain was one big prison; and so were the ghettos of the Middle Ages."

In Pawlak's story, this protestation was answered by "the commander" of the developing ghetto rebellion with the assertion that the day—April 19, 1943—was actually the day of freedom: "Don't you see that we are free? No longer do we listen to orders. They tell us: Come out of your hiding—and we refuse to come out."

I read such accounts, note such histories, and pray that such rationalizations perhaps made dying somehow easier for the victims of the ghettos, the camps, the murdering fields of Europe. It is a matter of record that the beginning of the implausible Warsaw ghetto revolt coincided with the arrival of Passover, April 19, 1943. While I certainly believe in the realistic report of Wladyslaw Pawlak and others that so many Jews regarded the timing as further evidence of their unrelenting tragedy, I also allow myself to believe that the presence of the freedom holiday did give some strange structure, even some spiritual format, to their torment. When grief is unspeakable, is there not some bit of solace, some release in converting the grief into an old liturgy? Is there not some grisly truth in the language of a child who articulates an entire people's pain by asking: "And why do we have neither leavened nor unleavened bread this night?"

They obviously knew they were going to die. They were so sure of it that they chose to die fighting the Germans with makeshift bombs, flaming bottles, and some rifles stolen from German corpses. Better this death— even for their children—than as slaves in a concentration camp. I allow myself to believe that the arrival of Passover—even the twisted entrance of the Angel of Death— helped frame the bravery of these few hundred Jews who turned the weeks just following April 19, 1943 into an extended Passover of the martyrs. I permit myself to think that the reality of the Passover—though profoundly bitter—helped to inspire the attitudes of so many sewer-bound "commanders" who, in one way or another, insisted: "Don't you see that we are free?"

It is exactly their heroism, their undaunted appropriation of the holiday into their greater will to die with dignity at the worst of times, that brings me the answer to the question: What's the point of Passover after the Holocaust? If *they* did that at Passover, then *we* should learn at Passover to live with dignity in these best of times. If they had no matzoh, no wine, no hope, and no life on Passover eve, then we should learn to cherish such things in the luxurious safety of our Passover eves just over a half century later.

At the most mundane of levels, we should learn that Passover prevailed in the Warsaw Ghetto. Jews certainly died; Judaism did not. Had the Germans truly achieved their goals, there would be no matzoh, no wine, no learning, no songs anywhere. There would be no books about Passover, no scrolls of Torah, no questions, and no answers. There would be no grandmother revealing her secret recipe for matzoh balls, no uncle slyly hiding the *afikoman*, no children reciting the Ten Plagues. The fact that somebody kept the Passover, or, for that matter, decried the Passover during such dark times and horrifying places tells me that the tradition itself liberates us from even the worst oppression. The very fact of Passover specifically, and Jewish practice generally, proved that April 19, 1943, was not a coda, but a difficult pause in the composition.

The truth is that Passover is about survival—and how we survive as human beings. I suppose that some people, looking at the bloody pages of Jewish history, could argue that we would have been better off staying in

Egypt. Some of the outgoing Hebrew slaves made this argument themselves. "Better that we should remain in Egypt," they murmured during some of the desert crises they experienced under Moses. "At least there we knew what each day would bring, and there was a guaranteed ration." Maybe, one could reason, the Jews would have been less vulnerable to national agony had we not become an independent nationality.

But life is about growth and practice. Only a people who experience things can teach its children with any insight. Only veterans of life—and risk—can truly respond to the questions that children are required by the Seder and inspired by life to ask. As the Passover story itself reveals, the Jewish people have had to deal with much more experience than has been fair, reasonable, or even sane. There is no rationalization for Pharaoh's Egypt, Haman's Shushan, Vespasian's Rome, Isabella's Spain, or Hitler's Germany. Nor is there any such rationalization for today's Bosnia; the Jewish people, though veterans of genocide, are not exclusive in the category of victims.

But the Jews, starting in Egypt, scattering out from Judea, somehow surpassing Warsaw, Treblinka, and Auschwitz, have brought the question of survival to the discussion with unique ability and stamina. Passover did not die in April 1943; it will be here in April 2043. Rabbi Leo Baeck, known as the "Teacher of Theresienstadt," who guided fellow inmates of the so-called "paradise camp" from all faiths and persuasions, and who survived five inprisonments during the war, perceived this quality. Rabbi Baeck, who is said to have somehow produced a fresh tablecloth for many a forbidden Sabbath and Passover celebration in the midst of the concentration camp, wrote even before the war: "Israel understood that *existence, too, can be a mission;* the mere perpetuation of self became a sermon preached to the world." Isn't this more or less what the uncommonly brave sewer rats of the Warsaw Ghetto were asserting by their actions on Passover eve of 1943?

Baeck, who was the leader of German Jewry, reminds me of another teacher. Don Isaac Abrabanel was the leader of a different condemned community, the Jews of Spain, at the end of the fifteenth century. He often asserted the equality of human beings, "for all of us were impoverished in Egyptian bondage."

Don Isaac, like Leo Baeck, would have to live out his Passover analogy. When the paranoid Spanish monarchy expelled the Jews in 1492 (the same year Christopher Columbus was commissioned by Spain to find a new world), Don Isaac was offered an exemption from exile. He refused to be separated from his people. He experienced their Egypt with them, just as Leo Baeck would five centuries later. The fact is that Passover teaches us— particularly after the Holocaust—that we cannot separate ourselves from human anguish and hope in order to truly remain human.

Rabbi Baeck's story of survival is especially poignant. His biographer, Albert H. Friedlander, records an incident of remarkable fate. The Nazis wanted Rabbi Baeck to die in the camp; he was widely known and beloved as German Jewry's leading theologian. It turns out that a certain Rabbi *Beck*, a different cleric altogether, died in the camp just after Rabbi Baeck's arrival. The camp administration was notified that Rabbi Baeck had expired. As Friedlander wrote: "Overefficiency betrayed the oppressors. . . . Now [Leo Baeck] really was just one more number in the grim lottery of death; and, by a miracle, it was one of the few not drawn."

As it turned out, Rabbi Leo Baeck became one of fewer than 9,000 survivors of Theresienstadt among the approximately 140,000 Jews who were ultimately sent there. He survived by being inconspicuous, loving, supportive, and assertive about Israel's mission even when Israel was disappearing. He was to his people like a kind of Elijah the prophet—who enters the realm of the Passover table at the closing of the evening with a promise of redemption and guidance.

In Albert H. Friedlander's words, Baeck maintained himself as "a center of moral resistance." He taught forbidden, overcrowded classes, at odd hours, in subjects ranging from Talmud to Plato. He responded to cruelty with ideas—which is exactly what the Passover seder does for the modern world.

Yes, some people have asked, what's the point after the Holocaust? To some, the Seder may appear to be an archaic, silly ritual that throws miracles, games, and songs at the reality of human bestiality. They find the Hebrew prayers incomprehensible, the English locutions awkward and overbearing. They scoff at the notion of Elijah "appearing" at every Seder, deriding it as being as childish as the improbable, simultaneous sliding of Santa Claus down every possible chimney on Christmas Eve. They don't like magic tricks claiming a place in their holiday devotions; they take a dim view of the wine in Elijah's cup "disappearing" out of "his" goblet. They really wonder if there is any escaping the improbable odyssey described in the old story. It seems like Pharaoh is not only still with us, but that he is particularly carnal in the twentieth century.

Like anybody else, I think a lot about these things. I think about Leo Baeck teaching a bit of Greek philosophy in the midst of discreet candlelight in a place that even God seems to have forsaken. I think about the little Jewish children of France who were systematically separated from their parents and siblings, packed into dark cattle cars, and shipped to the gas chambers of Auschwitz from the Le Bourget station in Paris. I think about Berlin's Anhalt railroad station, site of so many deportations, now a memorial, which is still being vandalized and desecrated today. I think about the grandmothers of Romania, torn away from their sweet-smelling kitchens; the aunts and uncles of Lithuania, who were burned to death in their own synagogues; the parents and children of Kiev, who were marched into the forests of Babi Yar and killed together in ditches they themselves were forced to dig. I think about April 19, 1943, when my people contemplated the coming of both Passover and the S.S. storm troopers. And I myself wonder, what's the point after all of this?

Maybe the answer is found in the Haggadah itself. The Seder book, a kind of public diary of national allegory, nevertheless includes some direct reflection on the Jewish experience. Not too long before the demonstration of the Ten Plagues, during the section called *Maggid* (meaning "Narration"), the gathered assembly raise their cups of wine but leave the wine untasted. A passage is read, usually by the entire group: "We praise the God who keeps faith with the people Israel. God's promise of redemption in ancient days sustains us now. *For more than one enemy has risen against us to destroy us. In every generation, in every age, some rise to plot our destruction. But a divine power sustains and delivers us.*" (Emphasis mine.)

Some reference to, or selection from, Holocaust literature at times follows this declaration. For example, *A Passover Haggadah* of the (Reform) Central Conference of American Rabbis attaches a fragment of Anne Frank's immortal diary to this section. The *San Diego Women's Haggadah* includes the bittersweet story of Hannah, a Holocaust survivor who, as a young woman, was "dragged out by her hair" by soldiers while lighting the Sabbath candles with her family. She lost her family, but lived to have grandchildren in America who found their own "liberation" by being able to do creative work.

One Orthodox edition points to the fact that the text does not read that God *delivered* us. In an oblique reference to the ongoing reality of anti-Jewish outbursts, this Haggadah emphasizes that the text specifically reads that the deity *delivers* us—meaning that rescue and redemption are not static to the Egyptian bondage, but as current as the twentieth century. The Orthodox *Art Scroll Haggadah*, perhaps carrying this explanation too far, argues in its commentary that "we receive God's help *because* enemies rise against us in all ages; it is their inveterate enmity that has helped us, by gaining God's protection. Their hostility may, in fact, be a blessing in disguise."

I myself cannot live with such a rationalization of organized cruelty against any people. But I do appreciate the unabashed recognition of evil that appears in the Passover book, and that helps to bring the relief of heaven to the absurdities of the earth. The fact is that the story of Pharaoh and the Hebrews is as old as ancient Egypt and as new as the Iraq of Saddam Hussein. The fact is that when we contemporize the Exodus story around our dining room tables, we help to bring meaning to those events of the twentieth century that would defy any meaning. By making the Holocaust a reality, we not only honor the victims, but we dignify the desperate prayers said around barren Seder tables on April 19, 1943. And when we share all of this with our children, we are effectively teaching them that when someone is mean as a child, he or she can become murderous as an adult. Unbridled contempt now can lead to ethnic cleansing later; we need only consider the televised insanity of Sarajevo in the 1990s if we have any doubts about that.

No, the Haggadah does not act as if Egypt was some isolated incident that took place in some remote context. The Haggadah is about human nature, and about how human nature has caused a lot of pain. After the Holocaust it brings home a particularly urgent message: "Go and learn," it declares—about what people can and will do to each other. This is exactly the time, it seems to imply—as the twentieth century at last recedes—*not* to abandon faith and certainly not to abandon one another.

Nor does the book mince words about the difficult problems that have attended the story of the Jewish people in every century. Every Seder includes these rather cryptic words, taken from the Book of Deuteronomy: *"My father was a wandering Aramean, and he went down into Egypt, and lived there as a stranger, with small numbers."* The implication is that isolation is a parent to the Jewish experience. Even though the account in Deuteronomy goes on to tell how the Hebrews grew in number, "mighty and numerous," nevertheless the Egyptians "were cruel and afflicted us with hard labor." Is this the city of Ramses, or is it Warsaw? Are they not one and the same? A slave is a slave, even as human beings have always had the capacity to denigrate one another.

The Passover Haggadah draws from the past to enlighten the future. We see that the Hebrews eventually rebelled against their degradation and quit Egypt. We see that Don Isaac found dignity in his solidarity with the greater body of Israel who endured the exile together. We see that Leo Baeck found strength in huddling with his brethren, offering them the comfort of study and ritual in the midst of the kingdom of death. We see that, in her supreme isolation, Anne Frank found the wherewithal still to believe in the basic goodness of most human beings. We see that the Passover seder is a table set with order in a world of much disorder.

In the end, what is the answer to the question: What's the point of Passover after the Holocaust? We start with the fact that the very meaning, in Hebrew, of the word *Seder* is "order." Every Haggadah presents a list of the sequence of the service somewhere in the front matter of the book.

I remember well: At Passover my great-grandfather Yitzhak, a denizen of British Palestine who lived through the years of the European genocide and then witnessed the rebirth of Israel, read the "order" out loud with special solemnity. I was present only once at a Seder with the old man; his sea blue eyes shone above a thick white beard. I remember well that my great-grandfather declared emphatically: "Whosoever thinks he can change the order of the universe, let him come and hear the order that God has established from the very day our people fled Egypt." I thought then, and I believe now: If people would just eat in order, bless in order, love in order, then maybe we would finally find killing one another out of order.

In the midst of all the chaos of life today, *against the very disarray of society*, the Passover ritual rescues us, with its delineation, its rhythm, its innate discipline, its sense of history, its symmetry. In a society that disposes of everything from razor blades to celebrities, the Seder meal is organized, segmented, and, above all, revered. At a period in history when so many of us feel that we are rushed, harried, and overprogrammed, Passover returns every year with its reassuring promise and delivery of relationships, memories, and temporal peace. In a civilization where so few things are truly remembered, the Seder does not allow you to forget. At a time when there is so much illiteracy, actual and spiritual, the Seder calls every one of us to read, to contemplate, and to cherish a distinguished and informative recollection. At a time when we have so much information, but know so little about one another, the Seder restores family connections. It is something that is fathomed and measured in a world that is unfathomable and immeasurable. At the conclusion of an unreasonable century, the Seder brings reason, after all. It represents a concept, set against times that can hardly be conceived. The point of the post-Holocaust Passover is that beauty and song and affection and tenderness and harmony survived the genocide and will not be appropriated to the darkest side of this century, which already took too much from the human family.

In *Gates of Freedom: A Passover Haggadah*, by Chaim Stern, a concentration camp inmate is quoted in a remembrance of Rabbi Ephraim Oshry, who was also in the camps. Rabbi Oshry, like Rabbi Leo Baeck, believed that a supreme form of resistance was the act of studying and praying, exactly there, in the midst of hell. Evidently, somebody asked the rabbi if saying a blessing was even worthwhile in the environment of the death camp. The question, in fact, was focused on an old Jewish blessing that thanks God "for not making me a slave."

What was the point of such a blessing when, in fact, the Jews were surely slaves to the Germans? Rabbi Oshry was quoted to respond that, more than ever, the Jewish people should recite such a hallowed prayer. He exhorted his fellow inmates to perceive themselves "not as slaves, but as free people, prisoners for the time being, whose liberation will soon come." In such a view of themselves, Rabbi Oshry believed, was the finest and purest repudiation of their enemies and the greatest validation of themselves. This was the ultimate refutation of chaos—the reapportion of order.

Who could know about such a thing and not instinctively know exactly what the point of Passover is after the Holocaust?

## Chapter Five

# From Moses to Martin Luther King, Jr.: Passover and the American Dream

I n 1993, a well-known American journalist introduced a new book he had written with the following recollection:

> *As a seven-year-old second grader at the Bernard School in McMinnville, Tennessee, I went to the compulsory assemblies where every few days we would sing this spiritual:*
>
> > *"Go down Moses*
> > *Way down in Egypt Land*
> > *Tell old Pharaoh*
> > *Let my people go!"*
>
> *I'd barely heard of Moses in my Methodist Sunday School, and had no idea who Pharaoh was. But I got the sense that I was singing for the release of some people from bondage—black people, I supposed.*

Carl Rowan, the author and journalist, was introducing his biography of Justice Thurgood Marshall. Remembering his segregated school days, Mr. Rowan added, "I would later learn that the spiritual referred to the Children of Israel but was universal in intent."

With many African-Americans, the religion that they learned and grew up with, the faith that sustained and inspired them through much difficulty and anguish, is grounded in the Hebrew scripture. Specifically, the freedom ideology of so many Americans from a variety of ethnic backgrounds hails from the Passover saga of the Book of Exodus. As one Baptist minister in my community has told me several times, "We both have had our Egypt."

There is much to be said for this important sharing of a tradition, especially in these times of so much cultural division in our society. After the defining days of the civil rights movement, during which time many Jews transferred the meaning of the Passover story directly to their experiences as American citizens, there has been a most regrettable lapse in the relationships between Jews and blacks. We don't seem to share either an Egypt or an America. This is lamentable because society is not pushed forward in favor of social justice, and the Passover legacy of freedom-fighting remains somewhat in limbo.

When one reads the Haggadah, however, one reads about a universal yearning—for men and women to go free. This is something Jews and blacks do understand together, when both groups are willing to share. In the 1950s and 1960s, Jewish people often verbalized the connection during their Passover deliberations. They would have smiled upon Carl Rowan's recollection. These days, although many of us still think about how Passover's themes are meant to shape our relationship to society, some of us are apt, tragically, to resent a black writer's appropriation of "Let my people go!"

Passover makes me think about this tension. I don't want the old Egyptian story to remain static in the book, or to be forgotten as some ancient adventure that means little for my time, my community, my children. And in my lifetime there have been triumphant moments, from Birmingham, Alabama, to Pretoria, South Africa, during which people of many different colors have somehow lived out the historical refrain of "Let my people go!"

And so I think about what Passover says to blacks and Jews. Although we are two peoples who have failed to feel totally comfortable together, two peoples who have found a kindred spirit less because of a real affinity and more because society as a whole has fused us in its contempt, we nonetheless seem historically linked in American history. From Moses to Martin Luther King, Jr., we have been reciting some of the same poetry, we have been sharing dreams, we have found mutual strength, and we certainly have had much in common to fear when America as a whole has felt threatened by real or imaginary social and economic ills.

There is a Pharaoh of the spirit that comes to afflict both of our peoples. We are both intermittently blamed, or scapegoated, when something goes amiss in the general society. When a terribly sick white mother in South Carolina reported that her two small children had been kidnapped by a grisly black assailant, white Americans (including Jews) shook their heads in mutual confirmation that of course the perpetrator was a black man. It turned out that there was no such criminal; the mother had herself driven her own flesh and blood—strapped in their car seats—into a cold lake to be drowned. She murdered her own children, and by playing upon our worst instincts, she managed to denigrate our civilization.

When a referendum on secession from Canada narrowly failed in Quebec in 1995, the premier of the restless province promptly and bitterly blamed the defeat on "wealthy and ethnic minorities." The Jews of Montreal, Hull, and Quebec City didn't need a translation from the premier's French. The fact that the separation conflict of Quebec has nothing to do with the Jews (who themselves were split on the vote) and everything to do with history, language, and other social factors of North America seemed to elude the Christian leadership of *la belle province.*

There is a message in the Passover story that any cultural group could well afford to comprehend. It's simple: Slavery is bad; freedom is good. These two opposite conditions are contemplated by the Passover story in every dimension—physical as well as spiritual. An old Hasidic proverb reminds us that "the real slavery in Egypt was that they had learned to endure it." A poem from England intuitively tells us: "My very chains and I grew friends / So much a long communion tends / To make us what we are."

I think that I understood the psychological implications of endured, long-term degradation when, as a child,

I once saw it at a gasoline station in northern Florida. My parents, my younger brother, and I had pulled up to the fuel pumps en route home from a vacation in the South. Another automobile appeared at the same time carrying a black family. First off, the attendant summarily ignored the other vehicle and responded only to us. (What if he had known that mine was an immigrant family from *Israel*?)

Even more indelible is my memory of what happened next. My father took my brother and me to wash up. From the other car, another father emerged with his son. *We* went to a sparkling clean rest room that, to my extreme discomfort, was marked WHITE. The other father and his boy went elsewhere. I saw the look in their eyes as we separated in front of that miserable service station. It was the look of learned slavery. That dad and his son—who was more or less my age—are part of the unwritten text of my private Haggadah forever.

When Moses went into Pharaoh's court and demanded freedom for the slaves, he was speaking for every nation and for every epoch. This was the first time, in the recorded history of humankind, that any cultural group had demanded and eventually got a deliverance from the confines of another cultural group. This is also the first recorded religious tradition alleging that even the heavens intervened in the matter of slavery versus freedom. Over and over again the Bible tells us that God "heard the cries of the Hebrews." Whether or not you interpret the scriptural assertion literally, the fact remains that this is the original saga linking the intention of heaven with the direction of earth. And, indeed, Moses was the world's first civil rights leader, and the Hebrew exodus from Egypt was the world's first national liberation movement. No wonder that many American Jews, among other good and courageous people, identified with Dr. Martin Luther King's social revolution of a generation ago.

The partnership of Jews and African-Americans in the era of the freedom marches produced benefits not only for the indigenous black victims of Southern segregation. Fulfilling the Passover admonition to understand the suffering of others because "we were strangers in Egypt," the Jewish community joined its forces and its energy to the civil rights movement. What we need to remember, however, is that our involvement—besides being the morally correct choice—gave a great deal back to us as individuals and as a community. We might wish to ponder this while reading the Haggadah to our children.

When our social activists made their way down to Birmingham, Selma, and Jackson, they were fulfilling their own idea of what Judaism is meant to be. The biblical prophets, from Isaiah to Amos to Jeremiah, mandated that we practice a national religious life based less on the rituals and *more on the acts of justice* that repair the world. Isaiah was particularly scornful of Jewish life that offered up vacuous rituals and empty fasts devoid of meaning. He would have had difficulty with people who wash their hands at the Seder but never cleanse their souls, who set aside the *afikoman* but never consider society's hungry, who light the candles at exactly the precise moment but never take the time to make some light against society's darkness. It's one thing just to read the Haggadah; it's another thing to live out its words. The prophet Isaiah paraphrased this concept a long time ago:

> *Is not this the fast that I have chosen?*
> *To loose the fetters of wickedness,*
> *To undo the bands of the yoke,*
> *And to let the oppressed go free,*
> *And that ye break every yoke?*
> *Is it not to deal thy bread to the hungry,*
> *And that thou bring the poor that are cast out to thy house?*
> *When thou seest the naked, that thou cover him,*
> *And that thou hide not thyself from thine own flesh?*
> *Then shall thy light break forth as morning.*

Indeed, the plight of black Americans cleared an avenue of spiritual meaning for many Jews at the time who were, frankly, not otherwise engaged by their Judaism. While we helped blacks to desegregate drinking fountains, to unlock the doors of state universities, and to open up voting booths, they in turn were opening up our Jewish souls and helping us to negotiate some of our own religious ambivalence. They—these victims of American racism—became our unlikely partners in the realization of our Passover promises.

In general, it was science and justice, not faith and spirituality, that defined those heady days of the Great

Society and the War on Poverty. Jews thought much more about the effect of the Soviet Sputnik than they did about the impact of the Jewish Sabbath. The European ashes of fascism were still fresh in the earth; no one dared to disturb them with too many references in the Haggadah or with a motion picture about what the Nazis had done.

In those days many Jews were particularly invested with philosophical questions about society, and with making sure that Jews fit in—assimilated—into the overall fabric of society. Religious rituals were not demonstrated too loudly; socially redeeming ideas counted more. Rabbis mixed quotations from Ezekiel with the poetry of Gandhi; they scrambled to draw a line—and it was a legitimate one—from Pharaoh to George Wallace. In a sense, the Passover story was a year-round proposition for Jewish practice; its themes and sensibilities helped define our community in the day and age of Martin Luther King, Jr.

Indeed, the chant of "Let my people go!" was not so much a cantillation as it was the political plank of almost every synagogue and Jewish agency back then. In the spirit of a timely conciliation, it should be noted that Jews did not just give to blacks in those important days; blacks gave to us as well. Frankly, the needs of African-Americans provided Jews with an agenda long before our more recent infatuation with rituals, with the Hebrew language, with Jewish literacy, and continuity. The typical American Jew a generation ago knew a lot more about Martin Luther King, Jr., than about Oskar Schindler.

I refer to all of this for two reasons. First, the awareness of Passover values, usually learned around a Seder table, clearly motivated many thoughtful Jews to participate in the modern American social struggle against the Pharaonic sheriffs, mayors, and governors of the old Confederacy. Second, given that the spirit of this involvement has truly waned in this era of black–Jewish confrontation, it is worthwhile to revisit the real parallel between the two "Egypts."

I would like to venture into the Bible—where the freedom story originated. When it was the Hebrews who were about to be liberated, there was a designated leader and there was a destination. Our fathers and mothers in Egypt were released into a religious tradition, and they were headed for a specific land inheritance. The Hebrews were delivered together, they were handed a series of defining laws, and they were transferred to a holy plot of soil. This Passover account is the historical body psyche of the Jewish people.

"Let my people go" did not ring so truly for the African-American slaves of this continent. They were delivered by an Emancipation Proclamation agreed to by only half of a nation embroiled in a civil war. There was no equivalent convocation following manumission at any kind of Sinai. Black Americans were freed—to drift off and hide. Unlike the Hebrews, they were not given a legal code to help them become citizens, or even participants, in civilization. The cruel aftermath known as Reconstruction was hardly a redemption. As a group the former slaves of America were not led by Moses. They were chased by another fellow whose name was Jim Crow.

Yet the parallels, and the shared insights of a common Egypt, are startling and revealing. Every Passover we are actually able to apply a significant, fairly recent American passage into the text of our time-honored guidebook. There are even remarkable, if not poignant analogies to be drawn between Moses the lawgiver, and Martin Luther King the lawmaker.

Neither of these two men went looking for his mission. They were both reluctant prophets. When God charges Moses to return to Egypt from his quiet life in Midian and to confront Pharaoh about the Hebrew slaves, Moses is sure that he is the wrong man for the job: "But they will not believe me, or hearken unto my voice." Moses lacks the confidence, nor is he particularly ambitious for the assignment. He even pleads that he is ill-suited both to confront the Egyptians and inspire the Hebrews because of a physical impediment: "Oh Lord, I am not a man of words . . . for I am slow of speech and of a slow tongue." God assuages the diffident shepherd by assigning his brother Aaron as spokesman for the developing civil rights movement. Moses, however, after eventually being upbraided by God for his hesitation, would emerge as the moral center of the first recorded showdown between an oppressive government and a social movement for freedom.

Moses was understandably reluctant to leave the

bucolic fields of Midian, where he lived a good life with his wife and family. It should be noted, however, that he had come to this pastoral existence as a fugitive from Egyptian justice. Like Martin Luther King of the twentieth century, Moses had legal problems because of his spiritual conflict with profane laws.

Moses, through serendipity, was a Hebrew child who nonetheless grew up in the plush environment of the Egyptian palace. When the Pharaoh had earlier ordered that all Hebrew male children be killed, Moses was set afloat in his crib and rescued by, of all people, the princess. The well-known biblical tale is meant to teach us—in the spirit of Passover—that compassion can emerge even from within the camp of the oppressor.

When Moses grows up, however, he is torn by the truth of his heritage. He is, of course, protected from the bondage of his actual countrymen. But one day, seeing particular brutality against a group of slaves on the part of a taskmaster, Moses is overcome by both a sense of kinship and a vaulting rage. According to the Bible, he slays the Egyptian, and is forced to flee Egyptian justice. The destiny of his leadership is born in the fire of his overwhelming and ultimate identification with his beleaguered people.

In the fields of Midian he finds safety, tranquillity, and some peace of mind. That remains so until history (first in the form of the famous burning bush) intervenes, sending him back to confront the official demons in Egypt.

Martin Luther King, Jr., scion of a middle-class Atlanta

family, namesake and son of a respected preacher, also grew up somewhat removed from the experience of his fellow Southern blacks. Intellectually lithe, worldly, and cultivated, he excelled in graduate studies at Boston University. He earned his doctorate in an environment that few blacks—even as brilliant as he—knew or even understood in the years following World War II. But, like Moses, he was unable to disassociate himself from the tribulations of his people. Feeling a natural affinity, he deliberately took on a modest pulpit in Montgomery, Alabama. He chose a simple lifestyle and desired to preach his faith to regular people who brought their prayers, their milestones, and their heartaches to the Dexter Avenue Church.

But, like Moses, the conditions of society brought King his destiny as well. Montgomery, like all Southern cities in the 1950s, was officially and vociferously segregated. King was offended and angered, although he maintained his focus on his ministry. Like Moses, he tended to his family and to his flock. He sought only to be a shepherd, but a combination of factors—some would say divine factors—changed King's direction and, ultimately, the karma of this nation.

When on December 1, 1955, a seamstress named Rosa Parks refused to relinquish her seat to a white man on board a Montgomery city bus, King was called to lead the confrontation against the Montgomery city government. A movement, and its leader, were created. King was truly reluctant, paraphrasing Moses' plea that "they won't listen to me. Who am I?" Finally, he agreed to assume the presidency of the newly formed Montgomery Improvement Association. He spearheaded and personified a boycott, involving fifty thousand black people, of the Montgomery city bus lines. In the course of the boycott, Dr. King was arrested, threatened, physically assaulted, and his home was firebombed. Finally, the United States Supreme Court affirmed that Alabama's segregationist laws were unconstitutional. The buses in Montgomery were officially integrated on December 21, 1956; a modern Moses was leading a new national movement that was the Passover drama remade.

Dr. Martin Luther King, Jr., would eventually write: "Oppressed people cannot remain oppressed forever. The yearning for freedom eventually manifests itself. The Bible tells the thrilling story of how Moses stood in Pharaoh's court centuries ago and cried, 'Let my people go.'" Over the full and difficult years of 1955 to 1968, when King was murdered, the preacher, in fact, would be as Moses in the court opposite many Pharaohs—from Birmingham police chief Eugene "Bull" Connor to Alabama Governor George C. Wallace to Chicago Mayor Richard Daley.

There is no question that King associated himself with Moses, and that the Jewish people—who set the Seder table yearly—identified with King. In the 1950s and 1960s, a great many Jews, from all walks of life, would befriend him, support him, march with him. They knew his travail; they truly heard him. They found rich common ground between the way in which the Georgia pastor homiletically rendered an old Negro spiritual and how they themselves recited a biblical psalm. When they heard the reverend say, "Freedom is never voluntarily given by the oppressor; it must be demanded by the oppressed," they understood that this was another way of crying, "Let my people go."

In those days Passover was set free from the confines of the dining room table, and it floated and swirled about the towns and villages and courthouses and churches of America. Dr. King, of course, completed his personal analogy to Moses when on April 3, 1968, in Memphis— one night before his assassination—he offered an uncanny, prescient oration to his followers:

> *I just want to do God's will. And He's allowed me to go up to the mountain. And I've looked over. And I've seen the promised land. I may not get there with you. But I want you to know tonight that we as a people will get to the promised land.*

It was a remarkable night, a modern Deuteronomy, when Dr. King, hours before his death, enacted the biblical text near the very conclusion of the Five Books of Moses: *"And Moses went from the plains of Moab unto Mount Nebo.... And the Lord showed him all the land.... 'I have caused thee to see it with thine eyes, but thou shalt not go over.' "*

I believe that the spirit set by the holiday of Passover, so thoroughly relived in the American civil rights movement, permitted a person like Martin Luther King, Jr., to elevate his journey and even his vision. The truth was that King lived a short, brutal life, filled with prison stays, bouts of depression, fear, and threats. He had very little time with his wife and children; he was harassed by common criminals and by the Federal Bureau of Investigation. He was finally reviled by many of his allies in the federal government, including President Lyndon B. Johnson, because he ultimately took a strong moral position against the Vietnam War. He was practically a prisoner of his passion, was eternally exhausted, and was cut off before even attaining the age of forty.

One wonders from whence he drew his remarkable strength, his courage, and his indomitable faith. It might have been from his personal association of his life and career with the Passover story. While he drew great insight from the works of Mahatma Gandhi, and while he certainly was quintessentially the minister of the Gospel of Jesus, some distinct theme carried him through his intense, if brief, years of struggle and leadership. Dr. King was known to quote the Talmud often; it would appear that he *lived* the Passover texts of the Book of Exodus. In that sense his story and that of his great salvation saga were genuine echoes of the world's original freedom ride. America, like Israel, has had its Egypt.

But the story transcends the hills of Alabama and the valleys of Mississippi and the tenements of Chicago. It even transcends Egypt and Israel. The strains of "Let my people go" are as old as God and as new as this morning's newspaper. Verdi expressed them in his "Coro di Schiavi

Ebrei"—the Chorus of the Hebrew Slaves. Citing the universal longing for one's own native land, the Italian composer wrote:

> *In my dreams, I abide there forever,*
> *and around me my loved ones are thronging.*
> *Oh, my homeland, shall I find these never?*
> *Never more by the clear Jordan stand?*

And what did they mean in South Africa, when they dreamed the same dream of the Hebrews, which we Jews intone every spring? In *Singababambayo*, sung in Pretoria but known spiritually in Jerusalem as well as Birmingham, it is chanted:

> *On earth an army is marching*
> *We're going home*
> *Our longing bears a song*
> *So sing out strong*
> *Sithi Halleluya.*

In the end, when somebody asks about the absolute meaning of Passover, one can respond that it is, simply, a song of freedom that is confined to no heart and to no language. It just happened to have been spoken eloquently one day in a place called America by a man named King who recalled another man named Moses.

## Chapter Six

# So Why Is Moses Missing?

Having spent some time examining the central role of Moses in the Passover history, it is important to make note of something. Moses is conspicuously absent from the text of the Passover Haggadah. If you examine a traditional Haggadah very closely, you are unlikely to see Moses' name mentioned anywhere in the text. His name may be found occasionally in more contemporary editions, but not often. Since the more modern, or stylized, or interpretative, editions of the Haggadah still draw from the basic texts—where Moses is omitted—they generally subscribe to the lack of references regarding the key figure of the freedom drama.

This is one of the most remarkable—and edifying— absences in any literature. In a way it follows on a very old cycle of omission in the Jewish scripture. While we do sometimes refer to the Torah as the "Five Books of Moses," the fact is that not one of the five books is actually named for him (Genesis, Exodus, Leviticus, Numbers,

Deuteronomy). Not a single one of the weekly Torah portions is named for Moses, but that is not because of any prohibition concerning the use of somebody's name for these sacred sections of the Bible.

Noah has a portion named for him, even though he was not a Jew, and even though the rabbinic tradition carries mixed reviews for his moral character. There is a portion in Numbers named for Korach—a rebellious malcontent whose demagoguery almost destroyed the Children of Israel. There is also a portion in Numbers named for a heathen king named Balak, who hired a mercenary prophet to go out and curse the Hebrews. But there is no specific, dedicated section of the scripture in honor of Moses.

It's worth noting, however, that there is a section in Exodus named for Moses' father-in-law, Jethro. But not only was Jethro not a Hebrew, he was a Midianite and, in fact, was the high priest of that nation. The fact that any Torah portion would be named for a gentile priest is remarkable enough—even with his family connections to Moses. What is truly remarkable here is the fact that the particular portion named for Jethro (whose kindness and wisdom is celebrated in rabbinic literature) is the portion that contains the Ten Commandments!

So it would seem that nobody has a premium on celebrity status in the annals of Jewish writ. Nor are we meant to be haughty about our status as a people; God's foundation laws are given to humankind in the name of a non-Jewish cleric who happened to have been a very good man. All of this is meant to teach us something, even as the conspicuous absence of Moses tells us something about the ultimate equality of all human beings.

Jewish people are not always so sure about this. Passover has a built-in message of egalitarianism that is subtly served by the *lack* of focus on Moses. Jews are sometimes confused, or misled, by the notion of being the "Chosen People." We misunderstand what the mission of being chosen actually implies. Passover is an opportune time to revisit this concept.

We were not chosen to be *better* than anybody else. A tradition that includes an annual spring rite focusing on the immeasurable value of human dignity is not packaged with haughtiness. It is good to remember what we mentioned in Chapter 2, that the Passover book does not admonish "every *Jew*" to feel as though he or she had personally left Egypt. Even the most traditional text reads that "every *person*" is to associate with the freedom saga. There is an abiding message of equality that resonates throughout the Passover literature.

The Jewish people did not receive the Torah (specifically, the Ten Commandments) in order to keep it to ourselves! There is no proprietary relationship between the Jews and the scripture. We are the "chosen people" in the sense that we were elected to acquire the Torah for the express purpose of *sharing* it with the rest of the world. It is for this clear reason that we are admonished to be "a light to the nations." Any other interpretation of our "chosen" status smacks of exclusivity—and just doesn't square with the historical understanding of the events at Sinai. Again, the very name of the Torah portion that describes the giving of the Ten Commandments at Mt. Sinai tells us a lot about the egalitarian nature of the whole thing: This signal event is not named after Moses, or after any particularly Jewish person or institution. The foundation act of receiving the Law at Sinai is associated in nomenclature with Jethro.

We can also gain some insight from noting the very location of the revelation at Sinai. The Ten Commandments were not revealed to Moses and the Hebrews in downtown Jerusalem, in *yiddishe* Poland, or in any Jewish neighborhood, for that matter. The geography of Sinai has more to do with the human soul than with politics. The Law was revealed in an uncharted desert, in the open air, in a place that belonged to everyone and to no one. The universalistic intent here is underscored by these facts. Nor does the very language of the Ten Commandments betray any cultural or national bias. The majority of the laws are written to every person, with no tribal qualifications: *"You shall not kill; you shall not steal; you shall not bear false witness; honor your father and mother. . . ."*

The words "Hebrew" or "Israelite" or "Jew" or any specific group identification appear nowhere in the text of the Ten Commandments. So in case any Jewish student of history needs clarification on the glaring lack of exclusivity that there is for us regarding the status of being "chosen," he or she need only consider that the defining Ten Commandments were given outside political boundaries, without restrictively identifying language, and within a scriptural portion that honors the universalistic goodness of a priest who was not a Hebrew. Passover, bonding "every *person*" to the ideal of freedom, only reinforces this ultimately inclusive and democratic message.

Passover, in fact, is a gentle flash point for this old and enduring set of values. I note, with interest and pleasure, the inclusion of the civil rights ballad "We Shall Overcome" and the slavery-era American song "Follow the Drinking Gourd" in a Haggadah as traditionally oriented as Richard N. Levy's *On Wings of Freedom*. These, and the ecumenical "Down by the Riverside" are interspersed next to such proverbial Hebrew folk songs as "Do-Di Li" and "Lo Yissa Goy." At Passover, nobody's pain is more than equal to anybody else's. Nor is anybody's dream more precious than anybody else's. The Law of God is seen by the Jewish people as received by every human soul. Nor is any particular leader—even Moses—more human or less mortal than any one of God's children.

I remember, as a child in Israel, about the puzzle of Moses' grave. In grade school, our history textbook was the Bible—which is Israel's national story. We often set out on field trips, surveying the sites of the chronicles, planting trees, and singing hymns in orchard fields once walked by the likes of Joshua, Deborah, and Samson. I recall when our fourth-grade class visited the rocky bluff where David allegedly slew Goliath; a few of us scrambled to see if we could find any discarded slingshots.

In a similar vein was the frequent search for the grave

of Moses. We understood from the history that the site was deliberately unmarked *("... and no man knoweth of his sepulcher unto this day")*. A couple of us boys thought it would be most opportune to be the discoverer of the law-giver's crypt. I'm not sure what criteria or evidence in the fields would have suddenly pointed us to the ancient site; the speculation and the mystery were simply too tanta-lizing for practicalities. Moreover, if we had really paid better attention to the biblical details, Deuteronomy does reveal some of the coordinates of Moses' grave: *He was buried in the valley of the land of Moab over against Beth-peor.* In other words, the site is east of the Jordan River; the terri-tory of the state of Israel in 1961, for example, was clearly confined to lands west of the Jordan. Frankly, we never drifted anywhere near the burial site during those won-derful field trips.

But no matter. The ground beneath us tingled with excitement and meaning. The sky carried the whispers of prophets and kings. We could see the mountains of the Jordan Valley and think of the Hebrews coming home. We could gaze in the direction of Egypt and picture Pharaoh's stubbornness and Moses' grit. Our imaginations joined the history in a benevolent partnership that made our collective childhood rich with consequence and sweet-ness. Most significant, perhaps, was the absolute parity of our lives—even as we came from a variety of experiences and places.

My collaborators in the search for Moses came from Russia, from Poland, from Morocco, from Yemen, and from Brazil. Some of them were the children of Holocaust orphans; some, like myself, had parents who were born essentially free in mandatory Palestine. Under the biblical sun, just miles from the Sinai desert and the original freedom story, we were all simply children of the remnant.

It was altogether appropriate that we never found the bones of Moses. No one should ever come across the site; something entirely inconsistent with the spirit of Passover would surely result. Biblical Judaism, which loves the unadorned dramas of human life, which reveals the Law in a politically generic wilderness setting, which celebrates social justice, and which lamented the eventual anointing of kings in ancient Israel, would instruct us not to deify a human being. And that's what Moses was, after all. He was a man, flawed, hesitant, sometimes impatient, often wise and heroic. He got angry with his people and could carry quite a grudge against members of his own family. His ultimate crowning in the Jewish tradition has nothing to do with royal lineage; he is simply remembered as *Moshe rabbeinu*, "Moses our teacher."

We are not supposed to make men and women larger in death than they were in life. The fascinating absence of Moses from the Passover text tells us a great deal about Judaism's instincts concerning the human family. It also betrays a real problem with some of the disturbing dynamics at play in Judaism as the twentieth century draws to a close.

It was hard for many people to comprehend the

dangerous dynamism that led one religious zealot to murder the prime minister of Israel in 1995. "God told me to do it," claimed the assassin, who carried both a yarmulke and a revolver. But we came to understand that it was not God but a cadre of misguided, misguiding, and Pharaonic Jewish clerics who effectively told the young man to commit a heinous crime that sickened all decent peoples around the world. As we notice the elucidating omission of Moses from the freedom text, we can't help but wonder at the appropriation of Jewish text for themselves by religious fanatics who have truly forgotten that Moses is revered above all for his humility.

We all have strengths, we all have flaws. All people, including the Jewish people, carry elements of dysfunction. Good and evil are universal possibilities; no one is immune from mortality, and no one is to be exalted beyond his or her humanity. Everything about the Passover ritual underscores the value of human equality; it is even a reason given by the rabbinic tradition for the practice of reclining at the table. "We all recline," the Haggadah tells us, because we are all in the same position, regardless of social station, elected position, or celebrity.

I remember an occasion when a deputy ambassador of Germany, Thomas Matussek, came to speak in my synagogue in Cleveland. It was a milestone gathering—our annual Service of Remembrance in honor of the six million Jewish victims of the Nazi Holocaust. Mr. Matussek, who represents his government at their embassy in Washington, D.C., graciously accepted our invitation to address us at such a moment of intense and relevant dedication. He came and spoke plainly about the German crime. He acknowledged the six burning memorial candles that were lit on our pulpit, each one, as he said, "signifying one million extinguished lives."

We in our congregation thought that the diplomat spoke well and sincerely. We acknowledged his plea for the beginnings of a reconciliation between our peoples. We made clear our peculiar burden of memory in light of what the Germans had done so systematically and enthusiastically. Most of all, we remembered and cherished all the victims of the genocide.

Following the service, Mr. Matussek, with whom I developed a friendship, joined my wife, Cathy, and our daughters, for a little repast at his hotel. There we were— an unlikely crew of people enjoying some rest and reflection, sharing some coffee. We had all participated in a signal event that served to make some sense out of an incomprehensible history. The diplomat is about the same age as me and, as it turns out, also has two daughters. As we relaxed and chatted, it became clear that— even though he hails from Germany and I hail from Israel—we pretty much share the same anxieties and hopes at the end of the day.

Cathy and he compared notes on how she and Mrs. Matussek both cope with today's carpool culture. All four of the teenage girls between our two families apparently are whisked to and from theater and music lessons, library runs, the homes of friends. Both the Kamins and the Matusseks wonder about the best summer camp situations for our girls. Both sets of parents are wary of their girls' developing social concerns; both sets of parents dread the evolving years of driving cars and dating boys. All of a sudden it occurred to us that we are all, regardless of our situations, and the burdens of history, more or less in this together.

Perhaps this is what more thoughtful Germans realize was their nation's gravest mistake during those terrifying years. They made Adolf Hitler into more than a man; they permitted their darkest, messianic dreams to betray their very place in human civilization. No culture, including the Jewish people, will ever benefit from the extravagant lionization of any person, no matter how notable. When men and women lead, people will follow. When lions lead, people will die.

So when Cathy and I sat with Thomas Matussek, sipping coffee and exchanging family stories, the history of this century was hardly changed. Nor should it ever be— that was the point of the German diplomat's visit to my synagogue in the first place. But there was some inherent value to be gained when we realized that, at the end of the day, we all recline around the table.

## Chapter Seven

# Did God Really Hear the Hebrews Cry?

It was during the summer of 1979, while Israel was returning the Sinai Peninsula in increments to Egypt, that I had the opportunity to swim in the shimmering blue-green waters of the Red Sea and wonder to myself if this crystalline, biblical sea had ever really parted for the Hebrews and then closed over the Egyptians. My wife and I were leading a group of high school students on a five-week mission in the Holy Land.

Our expedition had made its way south, toward Sharm el-Sheik, the once and future Egyptian watching post at the Straits of Tiran. We had eaten flat bread with desert Bedouins, slept under the African stars, endured windstorms, climbed through wadis, observed soaring ospreys, and said prayers at the Monastery of St. Catherine and its strange, voluminous collection of human bones. We had ascended Gabul Musa—the traditional Mt. Sinai—arriving at the summit as the sun broke through and painted the pathways we were certain had been walked by Moses. Now, splashing in the Red Sea, gazing at its coral reefs and its countless fish, I could only speculate what the hot sun above might have possibly told me about what really happened here at the time of the original Passover.

As the story is told in Exodus, the Hebrews fled Egypt and headed in the direction of the sea. At its banks the former slaves faced their first group crisis. The expanse of what was actually called the Sea of Reeds (the additional 'e' was inexplicably dropped over time, leading to the new appellation, Red Sea) lay before them. They viewed the salty waters with dread. Meanwhile, Pharaoh and his chariots were raising the desert dust behind them. The terrified Hebrews were absolutely trapped in between two disasters.

Thereupon occurred one of the great interventions from heaven. God instructed a bemused Moses to climb atop a high rock on the coast. Moses was to raise his hands in a manner visible to the people. The waters of the sea then separated, allowing the nervous slaves to walk across the miraculous formation.

Meanwhile, the pursuing Egyptians reached the shoreline, gaping in amazement. Pharaoh, determined to recapture his fleeing properties, gave the order. The chariots would proceed along the dry breach in between the suspended waters. Of course, even as the Egyptians entered, the waters receded, drowning the entire company—an event laden with moral implications for the Jewish people that will be explored later in this book.

Was it a miracle as described in the Bible? Or is this the apocryphal reworking of a natural development? In 1995 two geologists named Omar and Steckler offered a theory about the scientific rift of the Red Sea. Their report appeared in a journal called *Science* and was summarized in the *New York Times*. I remembered my Sinai swim when I read it. The scientists pointed to a process called "apatite fission tracking"—the rising of the mineral apatite through cracks in the earth. The mineral contains varying degrees of uranium, resulting in a slowly evolving structural split.

According to Omar and Steckler, the original rift took place some 34 million years before Moses supposedly parted the waters of the Sea of Reeds. The geologists claim that the separation therefore already existed when Moses and the Hebrews came along 3,700 years ago. The rift is still widening at the rate of about a half inch per year. Perhaps Moses and his charges alighted at just the point of an evident, uranium-sparked partition of water and earth when the Egyptians were chasing them in the hours just following the original Passover.

In the sixth chapter of Exodus, God is quoted as telling Moses: *"I have heard the groaning of the children of Israel, whom the Egyptians keep in bondage."* On a number of occasions in this narrative, God declares a clear awareness of the anguish of the Hebrews, noting that heaven has heard their cries. At one point God says simply: *"Now you shall see what I will do to Pharaoh."* The Bible offers a dramatic series of events that prove God's direct interest in this matter: The divine hand punishes Egypt (and enlightens the Hebrews) with a cataclysmic pattern of plagues, parting waters, and ultimately a spectacular, mountaintop revelation of law and redemption. It's a great story forming the backbone of the narrative that we revisit during the Seder.

The question becomes: The power of the story notwithstanding, did it all really happen? Did God really hear the Hebrews cry? Did the Sea of Reeds actually part? Or, are we dealing with a remarkable combination of earthly, moral outrage and fortuitous scientific happenings that have melded into a powerful and didactic legend?

When we were children, and somebody opened a Bible, or a Haggadah, before us, we did not have to worry too much about where the words fit in history. There were no particular psychological barriers to cross; in fact, the adults around us, teachers, rabbis, parents, wanted us to enjoy a simple, fanciful relationship with the text. So, Adam and Eve came into our lives through the lovely Garden of Eden. Noah collected animals, two by two, and it rained long enough for the ark to float for forty days. Rebekah felt love for Isaac by the well, and Deborah wrote poetry that stirred men to the sentimental defense of the land of Canaan.

Of course, Moses rebuked Pharaoh, and the Hebrews went free—rescued by God. Moses then went up Mt. Sinai and received two tablets of the law. There was a pristine order to all of it, reinforced yearly by our visits around the Seder table.

The Bible is a library of good children's stories, but it is used by adults who are looking for answers in the categories of faith and verification. The fact is that, as adults, we need the Scripture in more powerful ways than we did as children. We need the text, at Passover, or on any day, to contain some truths for us so that we can be linked, through it, to the idea of a God. As children, we played with Scripture. As adults, we work with it.

Did God really hear the Hebrews cry? Did it really happen? For if we know for sure that it did, then we can close our eyes in a leap of faith, assured that there is a God who hears human voices. When we were children, there was no question about all of this. Now that we are adults, there sometimes seems to be no answer. At Passover, returning to an old text, and to old habits, we once again approach the enduring mystery.

In a sense, what we are really asking—as we consider the implications of the freedom story told in the Haggadah—is: Did the Bible really happen? In the 1990s, Torah study is on the increase; you discover people engaged by it in a variety of settings, ranging from synagogue libraries to corporate boardrooms. Attorneys and bankers and physicians are debating the personality of Joseph, the vanity of Solomon, the forbearance of Sarah, the reluctance of Moses—all the while wondering if these people ever actually lived, or if the examples of their lives can possibly offer insight in a hectic world quite a few centuries removed from Pharaoh's court.

Did it actually happen? What should be our relationship

to the biblical text—heavily recast in the Passover Haggadah? Does the text verify God?

Among some there is no doubt. The sophistication of
the late twentieth century has not only failed to dilute
their belief in the text, they even use science to prove it.

At a small academic center in the Old City of
Jerusalem, a group of believers mix Torah with computer
science. A recent edition of *The Jerusalem Report* described
the Aish Ha-torah yeshiva—a place committed to the
incontrovertible notion that God is the author of Scripture. For a number of years the yeshiva has promoted a
program called ELS. This stands for "equidistant letter
sequences"—found acronyms spelled out by Hebrew letters spaced at equal distances from each other in the text
of the Bible.

This is serious business for these people, and not a few
other literalists. Their computers have found the word
Torah itself in the very beginning sequences of Scripture. Starting with the Hebrew letter *tav*, at the end of the
very first word of Genesis (*breysheet*, "In the beginning"),
the succeeding Hebrew letters of the word Torah—*vav*,
*reish*, and *heh*—do appear at exactly fifty-letter intervals in
the text.

It may be a coincidence. But to those who live by the
fundamentalist notion that God's fingerprints live in the
text—and that God actually heard the cries of the Hebrews—it is a matter of earnest and wondrous revelation.

Some of these ELS findings do make you think. When
the computer was asked to find the ELS codes for the

Hebrew transliterations of the words for Hitler, Auschwitz, and Germany, something intriguing happened: It managed to locate these three words close to each other within the Genesis account of Noah and the flood. The connection between holocausts was bridged, and rationalized, for these sincere scriptural scientists.

Now, it should be noted that even some Orthodox Jewish analysts are skeptical about this approach to the integrity of the Bible. You can believe that God is directly involved in the story—as even some liberal Jews do—but not be given over to a series of computerized formulas for proof. Confronted with this ELS science, some people would wonder why, if God had wanted to enclose revelatory codes in the Scripture, would God have done it in such a way that could not have been unlocked until after the invention of the computer?

To this the cybernetic believers cheerfully respond: God wanted the whole thing discovered *specifically* in an age of skepticism about the divine authorship of the Torah. There is no question, therefore, that God actually heard the cries of the Hebrews in Egypt, and then intervened directly. There is no question that God did actually make the declaration of Exodus, chapter three: *"I have surely seen the affliction of my people in Egypt, and heard their cry by reason of their taskmasters."* There is no doubt that God spoke and said to Moses, in chapter six: *"Now shalt thou see what I will do to Pharaoh."*

Of course, with respect to the assertion of the ELS believers, who claim that God enclosed certain truths that were meant to be exposed only in the age of word pro-cessing programs, one can't help but speculate. This would mean that while hearing the cry of the Hebrews, and then eventually transmitting the Ten Command-ments to Moses at Sinai, God already anticipated the computer chip and its true role in the dialogue between heaven and earth.

But long before the computer, there was the human heart. Evidence of this is manifest in the Passover story itself. What is more poignant than the cries of human beings who want to go free? From Adam and Eve to Moses and Pharaoh to you and me, the issue has been the same: How does God hear us? When is God revealed to us—not only in nature, but directly in the scriptural record that God supposedly left behind? From the prophets to the present, we parents, grandparents, neigh-bors, and friends have shared the same yearning. Did the Bible really happen, allowing some documentary evi-dence of God's tracks? Or is it all essentially a compila-tion of legends and folkways to test our imaginations and to move our Seders along?

It is dangerous to have too sure of an answer to this question. As I suggested in the introduction of this book, the power of story actually transcends the text itself. Rabbi Abraham Joshua Heschel once said that a person who only has the Torah doesn't even have that. History, archeology, and common sense all indicate that one should be neither too smitten with nor too withdrawn from the text. At the Passover table, for example, we shouldn't become so obsessed with, or so skeptical about, the literal questions of the text that we stop discerning the dreams of freedom that inspired the text in the first place. If we become so involved in whether or not God actually heard this or that plea, we might very well forget to hear the meaning of the plea itself. Whether we believe in the text literally or not, the whole festival is compromised if we don't believe in the message of the words. To put it another way, whether or not God was actually involved in the drama, the text dies the moment we stop wondering if human beings were involved in it. The letters of the Haggadah before us become rhapsody only when we let our hearts sing.

Meanwhile, if one is prepared to testify that the Scripture is the literal truth, then one has to contend with the evident contradictions in the text, or with the fact that some of the accounts in the document require God to be cruel, judgmental, arbitrary. What about the Tenth Plague that we mention during the Seder? Do we really want to accept that God murdered all the firstborn sons of Egypt—just to prove a point? How comfortable are we with the constant refrain in the Passover drama that God hardened Pharaoh's heart? On several occasions, and in order to prolong the cycle of the demonstrative plagues, God deliberately makes Pharaoh more obdurate—even though the king shows signs of softening and reneging on the question of freedom for the Hebrew slaves. If we want to anthropomorphically give over the Hebrews' cries to God's ears, then are we going to deposit some of the raging brutality of the Passover narrative directly in God's heart?

We have to understand that the Bible, like good leather, is characterized by flaws. There are, for example, two contradictory accounts of the Creation story, and there are two versions of the Ten Commandments—one in Exodus and the other in Deuteronomy. There are myriad inconsistencies in the details of the scriptural text, many revealed after the discovery of the Dead Sea Scrolls in 1947. In order to cope with the Bible's frequent skewing of time and logic, the rabbinic tradition adopted a prescriptive guideline to help in studying it: "There is no early or late in the Torah." We should not be too quick either to suspect or support the biblical text—except in the category of the human spirit. We're not exactly sure if the truth is that God directly freed the slaves, but we are exactly sure that freedom is the truth.

And if we lament the contradictions or the difficulties in the literal text, thinking that they deny the whole body of work, we should remember how the human soul works. *The power of the story* is what delivers Passover to us. People need legends to help religion fly; this has been true from Egypt to Greece to Israel to Rome to America.

If we accept that George Washington probably did not cut down a cherry tree, but still accept the national fatherhood of the first president, why would we accord less to Moses the lawgiver or to David the king? Whether or not Moses of the Passover saga actually made footprints on Sinai takes nothing away from what Sinai teaches us, or how the Passover sustains us. Whether or not David composed all of the psalms takes nothing away from their poetry. Indeed, the infighting over the literal involvement of such men or women in the works of Torah eventually undermines the way in which it works. When we come to the Seder table every spring, we don't first bring the letters of the Scripture as evidence of the holiday's vitality. It is ourselves that we first bring—our experiences, our pain, our insights. These take the letters off the page and distill them, with design, into the fabric of human lives.

The late and eminent Rabbi Daniel Jeremy Silver, who led my congregation in Cleveland for a full generation, wrote: "The text is not our homeland, life is." We can and should love the text, allowing the fresh air of our experiences to give it life beyond its parchment. Passover is also about the importance of interpretation, and it certainly is about asking questions! Indeed, there are manifold ideas about how you arrange the Seder plate itself—including "final" explications from such exalted and historical authorities as Rabbi Moses Isserles, the Gaon of Vilna, and Rabbi Isaac Luria. Your own grandmother probably had a pretty firm idea about this; I have always believed that Judaism flourishes because it is local. It has a lot to do with what your grandfather said to do with the wine cup, the challah, the spice box, the *afikoman*.

When we deal with the claimed literal veracity of any scriptural text, we must also deal with the literally hundreds of available versions of the Haggadah itself. First of all, we must realize that Passover came long before its manual. All the years that the Temple existed in Jerusalem, the people came with their sacrifices every spring while the attending priests of the Holy Temple sang praises. The idea of a Seder developed after the Romans destroyed the Temple in the year 70 C.E. The first signs of an organized Haggadah came during the ninth century; it evolved from a series of prayers, songs, traditions, and benedictions associated with the holiday.

Today there are countless, some dissimilar Haggadah editions, ranging from the *American Heritage Haggadah* to the *Birnbaum Haggadah* to the *Land of Israel Haggadah* to the *Polychrome Historical Haggadah* to the *A Singing Haggadah* to the *Sephardi Haggadah*. These are but a few examples of Orthodox editions. There are myriad Conservative, Reform, interpretive, art-based, feminist, gay, gender-neutral, politically correct *Haggadot*. There are some that are Holocaust-centered or Israel-based. For years there were editions set in the themes of the bondage of Soviet Jewry. There are some in paperback, others that are cloth-bound, some as huge as coffee-table tomes. They all certainly imply that God heard the Hebrews cry, but are not all prepared to agree on what that means or how it affected the more important conclusion that people felt compelled to seek and cherish the freedom.

Does it really matter if Moses actually climbed Sinai or not? Doesn't it matter more that the idea of cherishing a family, of respecting the human form, of sharing and preserving land, did indeed come down that spiritual mountain? When we sit at a Seder table, drawn together under the benevolent spell of story, does it matter more that God was somewhere three thousand years ago than that God is with us here and now? In other words, isn't the old story telling us that wherever God was yesterday, we have the responsibility to create God today—in our land, in our cities, in our families, in our times?

Judaism, like the evolving poetry of the Passover Haggadah, lives on its flexibility and resiliency. It has never survived by being frozen in one particular format, by remaining static. This is exactly why the Hebrews moved on from Egypt; the status quo of servitude was and remains unacceptable and libelous for us and for any element of the human family.

No, Jewish life, which resurfaces every Passover around steaming and spicy tables from Los Angeles to London to Amsterdam to Ashdod, has never survived in rigidity. When the pogroms came, we took our Torah scrolls elsewhere. When we were expelled, we translated our *Haggadot* into new languages so that the parents and children could always understand the story in their new land. We understood well what our medieval sages were trying to protect when they admonished us to turn over the text into the vernacular, in order for everyone to comprehend.

We were never trapped by our text; we molded it, lovingly, carefully, as we adjusted to new circumstances. Some of us have continued to believe that God has ears; others among us have been as equally concerned that men and women have hearts. We have benefited from all view-points. Perhaps this is why, when our people returned home to Israel in the freedom story of this century, we were able to build a new Sinai that blends tradition with the challenge of modernity.

We can argue all we want about whether or not God actually heard the Hebrews cry. We can even debate about what Abraham actually said to Sarah, what Deborah actually ordered her generals, what Moses in fact dictated to Joshua. Somehow, however, what links us to them—and their dreams to our Passover songs—is what they all felt. They appeared to experience a need to be touched by God. Our accounts of them, just like those of our family ancestors whom we visit or recall at Passover, is a loving blend of fact and faith.

For most of us, the question is not, did God actually hear the Hebrews cry? Better than the question, the answer for us is to give God something worthwhile to listen to, in our own day.

## Chapter Eight

# Biblical America: Our Own Ten Plagues

A remarkable thing about the Ten Plagues of the Bible, recited formulaically at the Passover table, is our basic detachment from them. We declare them and then pretty much forget them. Using either the edge of a knife or a fingertip, we ceremoniously place ten drops of wine on our Seder plates, but our connection to the ten-fold Egyptian crisis quickly dissolves into the chicken soup and beet preserves.

Chances are that during the course of the evening, Grandfather dwells more on the potential intoxication by four cups of wine than on the real infestation of countless beetles. The plagues—blood, frogs, lice, flying beasts, blight, boils, hail, locusts, darkness, and the slaying of the firstborn—are a litany of suffering and torment. Yet we itemize them without too much emotional involvement, and sometimes with a measure of impatience. For some it's an embarrassing and awkward moment—the ritual involving the utensil, the drops of wine, and the cantillation of exotic Hebrew words that paraphrase successive disasters all being a bit too pedantic for their taste.

Indeed, not all versions of the Haggadah have even included the formal declaration of the Ten Plagues. The original *Union Haggadah* of the (Reform) Union of American Hebrew Congregations, a slim gray volume held dear for decades, specifically omitted the ceremony. Bereft of too much Hebrew, compressed liturgically, the old *Union Haggadah* would not bear the plagues because their inclusion might have inferred an overbearing literalism. The revised edition of the Reform publication, released in 1974, includes the ritual of the plagues, replete with vivid artwork by Leonard Baskin. This edition also includes allusions to the Holocaust, the redemption of modern Israel, and other communal references shunned by the original volume. Still, the moment of the plagues is neither elongated in most current editions, nor dwelt upon, even as the ten drops of wine flow down the edge of the flatware—pulled more by gravity than passion.

I wonder about this. The Ten Plagues represent serious business, meriting our interest and attention. Are we so emotionally sanitized by the daily newspaper and television dispatches of intolerance, brutality, and despoliation that we receive such a history with noticeable dispassion?

It is worth looking at this problem from the point of view of language. The real implication of the Hebrew word *magafot*, meaning "plagues," comes from the root *magaf*. This olden word, meaning "to smite, to strike, to utterly defeat," is somewhat lost in the cosmetic and overused contemporary translation, "plagues." A typical expression, such as "I am plagued by lower back pain," does no quite match the biblical understanding of being victimized—as the Egyptians were—by a succession of poisoning, pestilence, and infanticide. I frankly prefer the occasional rendition of *eyser makot* used in some *Haggadot* to announce the ritual of the plagues. This phrase, more evocative than "ten plagues," means, literally, "ten hard hits."

Nevertheless, our benign involvement with the reality of the plagues continues. It is notable that in the Passover synagogue liturgy, a section called *Hallel* is shortened. The Hallel is a collection of praising poems, essentially drawn from the Book of Psalms. These jubilant stanzas are chanted at the seasonal festivals such as Sukkot, Simchat Torah, and Passover. The Hallel is somewhat curtailed at Passover—ostensibly in memory of the Egyptians who drowned in the Sea of Reeds after the plagues. It's an appropriate gesture born of the Passover tradition of empathy for the pain of others (which we will examine in the next chapter). But it remains more of a gesture than an ennobling tradition in terms of our comprehension of the totality of the disaster of the plagues.

The point is that we act as though the pattern of afflictions and trauma suffered by the Egyptians, and recounted systematically around the Seder table, was a one-time, unique affair—now dated and archaic. So what happened has become an isolated, blurry circumstance of ancient agony. Since so many of Passover's motifs, including the abhorrence of bondage and the dream of freedom, are continuously drawn from the text, it's a shame that we don't look at these plagues with eyes that are emotionally dilated.

The truth is that the Egyptian plagues, however caused, represent an ongoing cycle of human experience, exclusive neither to Pharaoh's subjects nor to any particular people in history. We endure the same plagues today—and then some of our own. An obvious example is AIDS. It is the plague of blood again, a curse of biblical proportions that, unlike the Egyptian plagues, is neither temporal nor even placeable in some historical context. One drop of red wine on a shiny dinner plate is hardly an expression of its unyielding and terrorizing presence in the fabric of our civilization.

Meanwhile, as we look at the biblical text of the Egyptian plagues, what was so unique about having waterways discolored by blood? The matter of a foreign substance infiltrating rivers and lakes is as much of a plague to us today as it was to the ancient residents along the Nile. Only now it is worse. Not so many years ago, the residents of Love Canal in New York, and of several communities along the Great Lakes, had no illusions about the First Plague. Hypodermic needles washing up along the beaches of American states, dangerous levels of lead in the tap water, and public waters contaminated by feces and general sewage are not a function of the biblical text. Such reports affect our lives today and tomorrow. If

Pharaoh were the king of Canada, would he not be plagued by acid rain and rust in his forests and lakes?

Are we to be complacent with respect to the frightening reports of the Second, Third, and Fourth plagues? What congeals the Egyptian disasters of frogs, lice, and beasts (including flies and beetles) when the states of California and Florida still cringe over the possible return of the Mediterranean fruit fly? Don't the people of Texas, Oklahoma, and even more northern points fear the creeping migration of the killer bees?

Meanwhile, to call the virtual saturation of New York City and other metropolitan areas by cockroaches and rats any less of a plague than the Egyptian incidents is to rationalize facts. We have our fair share of intimidating, dangerous environmental imbalances, from the bayous of Louisiana to the timberlands of Oregon.

The Fifth Plague, consisting of blight—specifically, livestock sickness—has direct parallels to today. The fluctuations on the index of beef prices is ample evidence. In the mid-1990s, a new level of concern rose in America about potentially fatal bacterias in meat that were killing people who ate hamburgers and steak sandwiches. Atrocious heat waves during the summer of 1995 felled thousands of innocent cows and bulls; what do we think, that this happened only once to Egyptian farmers? In general, the issue of animal malaise, and how it is so often caused not only by weather but also by human insensitivity or outright cruelty, represent a much overlooked plague condition.

What is so unique about boils on the skin, as relayed in the Sixth Plague? The authorization, a few years ago, for the sale of hydrocortisone acetate to the general public documents our own preoccupation with rampant skin irritations. All over America people are itching, scratching, cooling, wiping, moisturizing, soothing skin and scalps with topical and temporary gels, cremes, ointments, treatments, medications, and applications. Eczema, psoriasis, rash, skin cancer—we know from boils, only they don't go away.

When considering the cataclysmic nature of several of nature's recent seasons, we realize that the Seventh Plague, hail, was no isolated matter to be dismissed in a liturgical ten-count. Parts of the United States have endured especially brutal winters of late; over three hundred Americans perished during a particular season not long ago. It was hail back in Egypt; now it is often a fierce succession of hail, ice, sleet, water, and mud. The contemporary experience of the state of California can only have biblical connotations. I truly worry about California, where an uncanny series of rainstorms, mudslides, brush fires, deluges, earthquakes, and volcanic tremors have burned, flooded, and broken one of the most graceful confluences of seawater, hills, valleys, and vineyards ever designed by God. Trouble—in many categories—has hailed down on the Pacific coastline, from Mexico to British Columbia.

I sometimes think that the drop of wine associated with the plague of hail ought somehow be frozen for our modern understanding. But we'd have to be careful about which spirits to choose, because of the recent spate of Italian wine contamination, which followed the mini-plagues of cyanide poisoning and glass chips found in, respectively, our Tylenol tablets and our baby food.

The Eighth Plague, locusts, was only part of an ongoing cycle still affecting farmers and city dwellers alike. We need only consult with anyone who endures the cyclical swarm of cicada locusts. I remember each of their seven-year visits; they occurred while I was a youngster living in southwestern Ohio. There was barely a buckeye or oak tree in Cincinnati that was not engulfed by the homely, surreal cicada skeletons. The infiltration of bulging eyes and scary shells spread to our windshields, our doorways, and occasionally to the edges of our shoes. I understood—right in the middle of the twentieth century—what those Egyptian boys and girls must have felt like during the interval of their locust terror.

Meanwhile, the Ninth Plague, darkness, was only a shadow compared to the calamities of brownouts and blackouts that we typically endure. Some of these are caused by electrical transformers that either fail or are sabotaged. On other occasions, day is turned into night in some of our metropolitan areas by the Cimmerian haze of smokestack and automobile pollution. Meanwhile, when the "lights went out" in Egypt, the Bible does not record any looting or violence accompanying the cataclysm. We need only to read the newspapers to know that the coming of sudden darkness in our time is even blacker.

The death of the firstborn, Plague Ten, broke Egypt's official insensitivity to the Hebrew slaves and their yearning for freedom. In Cecil B. DeMille's epic motion picture *The Ten Commandments*, Pharaoh, portrayed by Yul Brynner, sits limply on his cold throne, holding his own lifeless son in his arms following this calamity. "Their god *is* God," he declares morosely. Even the seemingly callous Pharaoh apparently has a heart and a will that could be broken, at last. This was much more than a swarm of locusts, a bloodied Nile, or a batch of diseased cows. Children were dying, even as the Angel of Death swooped into the Egyptian homes while *passing over* the homes of the Hebrews.

Yet the declaration of this ultimate plague does not seem to change us. We mention the Tenth Plague as though it happened only there and then. But listening to Passover, one wonders: *What will it take to make the death of children an indelible plague for us to consider?* After Rwanda, after Bosnia, after Cambodia, after Lebanon, after Northern Ireland, after the Soviet Union, and after Nazi Germany, how can we simply discharge the tenth drop of wine and then move on to the imminent chicken soup and gefilte fish?

The Egyptian bloodbath was at least followed by a march to freedom. Today, we say *makat be-chorot!* (death of the firstborn) and buy handguns. In fact, several state governments have (in spite of the Brady Law) generally been making it easier to handle and transport guns in the past few years. The fact is that, according to the Children's Defense Fund, a frightening number of young children in American cities routinely carry, discharge, and are maimed or murdered by handguns these days in their schools, their playgrounds, their homes. This is not the tenth plague; it's the incalculable plague proffered by the looming Angel of Death who is revealed in gang colors, crack-culture music, and semiautomatic killing hardware.

In view of all this, and with respect to the notion that the Plagues are not isolated but, in fact, represent a continuum in human history, I have, for a number of years, proposed a special learning exercise for the Passover season. Since the message of Passover is timeless, and since we have agreed that the biblical text is not static but conscientiously renewable, why not seriously consider a discussion of today's ten plagues during the course of the Seder?

I remember when we added a large slice of covered matzoh to the center of the table in consideration of the beleaguered Jews of the former Soviet Union or of today's Syria in order to contemporize the historical message of the holiday. I have seen sections of matzoh, or fragments of liturgy, or special poetry included in the Seder to help us sympathize with the victims of AIDS, the sufferers of domestic abuse, the doomed children of Sarajevo and elsewhere. All of these meaningful rituals transform the rote recounting of the Egyptian plagues into the necessary and redeeming moral outrage of our own times. Such acts make us participants in history, not just readers of it. Such an attitude helps us, in the words of Professor Roger C. Klein of Cleveland, "move history into ethics."

Why not broaden the sometimes languid pronouncement of the Ten Plagues by having families and friends at home, or students in our religious schools, consider the question: What are ten plagues that you can identify as part of today's realities?

Think about it. You may improve a situation by considering the state of society in this way. I recall an anguished phone call from a congregant during the summer of 1996. America was in the midst of a series of suspicious fires that were destroying one African-American church after another; houses of worship were burning from the Carolinas to Oregon. "How can we stand by and do nothing, Rabbi?" agonized my congregant. "It's like one of the plagues of Egypt! Don't we have an obligation to care?"

In fact, the Jewish community had mobilized, through various of its social agencies, to help with relief efforts in the matter of the sinister fires. Like all decent peoples, we were outraged and concerned and not a little bit frightened. And to whatever degree we as individuals and as a group were galvanized to care and to help rebuild those houses of worship, the sensitization had something to do with our yearly immersion in the Passover text.

The reports and evaluations of "plagues" have a lot to do with cultural and historical contexts. Reading a list of old calamities from Egypt should be as edifying as our relationship to today's troubles and misfortunes and malpractices. What made the Egyptian plagues "biblical" was as much how they affected human lives as the fact of their canonization.

The esteemed Holocaust historian Lucy Dawidowicz once wrote about the mysterious and dreadful and peculiar circumstance that plagued the Ukrainian community of Kiev starting in the late 1950s.

The surviving Jews of Kiev, knowing of the horrifying mass massacres of Jewish families that took place at nearby Babi Yar, sought to sanctify the memory of these victims of the Nazis. The Communists, led by Nikita Krushchev, resisted the idea of a Jewish monument and instead elected to convert the fields of Babi Yar into a cattle pasture. They ultimately chose to extend the ravine there in preparation for the construction of a sports arena.

A dam was put up that was progressively raised every year. In her collection *What Is the Use of Jewish History?*, Professor Dawidowicz reported that on March 13, 1961, strong rains caused the dam to collapse. "Moments later, a thirty-foot tidal wave of mud poured into Kiev."

Houses and lives were swept away by the disaster. Old Jewish bones were washed up to haunt the lives of the Russians forever. Dawidowicz wrote:

> *In Kiev, people said: "Babi Yar takes its revenge." Peasants went to church to light candles and pray for the souls of the murdered Jews. Orthodox priests conducted memorial services*

*for the victims of the tidal waves and for the Jews killed twenty years earlier.*

In the matter of the Kiev tidal wave, when the earth spat up its Jewish corpses into the homes of those who denied their murders, one wonders: Was it heaven punishing, or just natural science unfolding? Only God knows—from Egypt to Rome to Israel to Russia to America. Surely, in some apocryphal document someday, the Kiev mystery will be recounted at some religious ceremony as the Plague of Mud. The 1996 church burnings of the United States may yet be recalled as the Plague of Fire. History and culture and rationalization and superstition and metaphysics combine into new traditions. What did the Egyptian plagues mean? How do they help us to identify our own? Thanks to the Passover heritage of inquiry, we are at least left to wonder, to learn, and, hopefully, to rectify.

## Chapter Nine

# Laughter and Anger in Heaven

Bosnians, Serbs, Croats: Not too many of us have been too certain about who is who, and who is fighting over what in that stricken, burnt, and bloodied corner of the world more or less known as the former Yugoslavia. What is certain is that terrible things are going on, even the specter of "ethnic cleansing." And when the president of the United States ordered that American troops make up a large part of a peacekeeping force for Bosnia, our reaction was generally tepid. We felt concern for the welfare of our soldiers, sailors, and aviators, but as far as the conflict itself, we just couldn't relate.

There have been intermittent moments of caring and anguish on our part concerning Bosnia. Every once in a terrible while, a bomb would blow up in a Sarajevo marketplace, killing or maiming scores of innocent people of all ages who had just been out shopping. A live report on CNN brought the shocking truth home to us; as conditioned as we have become to blood, we were momentarily appalled and sickened. But before long, pre-occupied as we are with our own problems, with the next "big story," or with a subsequent sports championship, the horror of Sarajevo would recede for us.

Passover is concerned with the virtue of empathy. Even the insidious bombing of a federal building in Oklahoma City was eventually shrouded in our memory by politics, Super Bowls, the O.J. Simpson affair, and by time itself. There seems to be a premium on vicarious emotion—especially when an individual or a group outside of our own immediate sensibilities is at stake or is being victimized by circumstances, opportunism, or even genocide.

An immediate legacy of Bosnia, apparent to Jews, is the denial of one of our favorite rationalizations about the Holocaust. For decades we maintained that if people had known about what was happening to the Jews, it would have been stopped. Or at least there would have been some noticeable outrage, some threat or gesture directed at the Germans, or implied in the matter of the eventual negotiations with the enemy who would surely seek some dispensation or "good points" from the Allies.

First of all, a lot of people did know. The Allied command made a conscious decision, for example, not to bomb Auschwitz even though it knew full well about the activities at the premier death camp of all time. The decision not to bomb was supposedly made for military considerations. We like to think that people did not know about the mass killings of the Jews and others, but there is overwhelming documentation that the opposite is true.

Nonetheless, we held on to the rationalization, for decades after the war, that the Final Solution was not challenged because it was basically unrevealed. The logic of this assumption is grounded in the hope of human empathy. If people had known, they would have done something to stop it. The Jews themselves were unable to grasp the enormity of the crime and to offer more resistance because, prior to World War II, and in spite of the dreadful history of European anti-Semitism, such ghastliness had never been perpetrated.

But in the matter of Bosnia, the facts of ethnic cleansing have been publicly known, telecast, and debated for years. For Jews it has been a topic of particular moral concern because of an old Passover covenant. Given that we were "strangers in Egypt," we must bear a particular sensitivity to the sufferings of others—even strangers. After Treblinka, how could *we* be indifferent to Sarajevo?

So now people clearly knew about a genocide in Europe. It was verified daily by satellite and videotaping eyewitnesses. But there was still no major outcry, no particular attempt to learn the facts or even help the countless, faceless victims. A sad, desperate exegesis about the murder of our own people was denied by the Bosnian combination of the media, the facts on the ground, and the prevailing failure of human nature.

It should be noted that during the Holocaust there were numberless examples of courage and sacrifice on the part of compassionate individuals who hid, rescued, nursed, or even just fed Jews. Nor must the noble efforts of the United Nations peacekeeping forces be overlooked in the matter of the Balkans. But in general, the twentieth century has betrayed the fact that human beings are not usually aroused to sympathizing feelings when brutality and bestiality is revealed—to whatever degree—against people we don't know or don't like.

Passover disavows such dispassion, and it crowns human sympathy. According to its folklore, the message comes straight from the heavens, and directly from Passover's own story.

Let us return briefly to the Ten Plagues—discussed in the previous chapter. We made reference to the custom of spilling one drop of wine onto the plate as each of the plagues is recited from the Haggadah. While this custom is time-honored, it is really not all that well understood. Some people associate the drops of red wine and blood— attributing sanguinary conditions to the various calamities. On the surface, this represents a bit of sophistry; the wine does not symbolize blood in this or any other Jewish ritual.

First of all, wine does not possess sacramental implications in Jewish practice. One of the tragic misunderstandings about Passover, exploited by Christian anti-Semites, is the notorious blood libel—the medieval charge that Jews required and used the blood of Christian children to help in the baking of matzoh bread. This was likely a corruption of the original, scriptural account concerning the blood of the paschal lambs that the Hebrews spread over their doorways in Egypt for protection against the advancing Angel of Death. As we shall discuss further in Chapter 11, some Jews hesitated using red wine at their seders for fear that some Christians would accuse them of mixing in and drinking blood.

A Jew drinks wine because it tastes good. We note the bittersweet flavor of the "fruit of the vine," drawing an analogy to life itself. When bride and groom share wine or grape juice at their wedding ceremony as "a cup of life," we pray that it will be less bitter and more sweet because they are sharing it together. The four cups of wine consumed at the Passover seder are inspired by the biblical text of Exodus, chapter six, verses six and seven: *"Wherefore say unto the children of Israel: I am the Lord, and I will bring you out from under the burdens of the Egyptians, and I will deliver you from their bondage, and I will redeem you with an outstretched arm, and with great judgments. And I will take you to me for a people, and ye shall know that I am the Lord your God."*

It just so happens that each one of the four cups of Passover wine represents one of the four key words in this proclamation of the liberation of the Hebrews from bondage:

1. *Bring out*
2. *Deliver*
3. *Redeem*
4. *Take*

So we should be clear on why wine is consumed in such a systematic, ultimately pedagogic manner during the Seder. There is nothing cabalistic or sinister about the Passover wine, although there is a wonderfully mysterious quality to the Cup of Elijah, as we shall eventually learn.

Meanwhile, no cryptic associations exist concerning the spilled drops of wine of the Ten Plagues. They represent neither blood nor witchery. What they represent is empathy.

We empty our cups of ten drops because our tradition finds it repugnant for us to enjoy a full cup while others suffered so much. The rabbinic tradition, in fact, made this a mandatory act of concern and sensitivity. Even if the recital of the ten disasters fails to alert us to today's various plagues and troubles, we at least are denied a full cup of joy in light of what the Egyptians endured. As Nathan Ausubel has so beautifully written, the motive for draining our cup of some of its drops of wine "was to caution the ethically conditioned Jew not to rejoice too much—not to drink the cup of triumph to its full in recalling the misfortunes that God had visited upon Israel's ancient oppressors, the Egyptians."

No, there shouldn't be too much haughtiness in the Jewish body psyche over the tragedies of others—particularly when our own good fortune is built on the foundations of those tragedies. The Egyptians were to be pitied, even if it was their own arrogance that indicted them. There's just nothing redeeming about the illimitable condemnation or mockery of a foe who has been vanquished. At Passover a scriptural proverb is often cited: *"Rejoice not when thine enemy falleth."* Meanwhile, the Talmudic parable that is found in so many editions of the Haggadah aptly summarizes Passover's call to empathy.

The parable has to do with the parting of the Red Sea, the escape of the Hebrew slaves, and the subsequent mass drowning of the Egyptians in their chariots. According to the rabbinic tradition, the ministering angels of heaven looked down upon this scene with great relish and exultation. God became very agitated that the heavenly hosts should view the unfolding cataclysm so subjectively.

The rabbis wrote that God conveyed his considerable anger: *"My children are perishing in the sea, and you are joyous?"* The mirth was stopped short in the heavens, and the situation was immediately regarded more soberly.

This little fable has meant as much to me all my life as anything else I have ever learned at or around Passover. It informs my outlook on life as a citizen of my country; it elucidates my view of Jewish social responsibility; it appropriately curtails my occasional infatuations with the notion of Jewish infallibility. It certainly reinforces my convictions—illustrated so vividly by the universalistic handling of the Ten Commandments in the scriptural text—that Jews are not very Jewish when we assume that God feels only for Jews.

In my own lifetime, it has helped me to view the Middle East conflict with a measure of regard for those who have been "the enemies." As a native of Israel, and the son of two parents who participated directly in the genesis of the modern Jewish state, I have no compunctions whatsoever about my birthland's historic right to thrive. The world as a whole has still not come to grips with the compelling and clear rightness of the existence of a free Jewish polity in the Holy Land—in light of history, and *particularly in light of twentieth-century history*. I feel the same moral certitude about the birth of Israel (with full United Nations sanction) after World War II as I do about the Hebrews' original march from degradation to dignity.

But the rabbinic tradition gave me a crucial and poignant caveat with the story of the laughter and anger in heaven. The message comes home again every Passover, whether or not the Haggadah edition I use at the Seder happens to include the tale. The very fact that the rabbis added this story via the Talmudic text—almost as though they carried an anxiety that the scriptural account of the Red Sea drama by itself didn't teach us enough—tells me a great deal about the ethical integrity of Judaism. Caring about the sufferings of others even when—or perhaps *especially when*—their sufferings move Jewish history along is something inviolate. Passover is about empathy; the rabbis would say it categorically endows everybody in the world as God's children.

Why did a group of Israelis—at great personal risk, as the eventual murder of Yitzhak Rabin proved—begin meeting secretly in Oslo, Norway, with representatives of the Palestine Liberation Organization in 1992? On one level, the Oslo agreements occurred because both sides simply realized that it was time to stop killing each other's children for yet more decades. Surely, there were practical, economic incentives involved, as is the case with so many international conflicts.

But for the Israelis, who have understood extremely well about being reviled and hunted across the chronicles of time, there was another dimension. So sure of our own righteousness, some of us had failed to ascribe the dimensions of humanity to the Palestinians and their history. Arab claims in this conflict, too often obscured by the incendiary actions of Arab extremists, can nevertheless be argued from a number of points of view, both new and old. The Hebrew Bible feels for the injustices endured by Ishmael; neither the Scripture nor modern facts can support anybody on some spiritual pedestal. *"My children are perishing,"* says God about the Egyptians in an old Jewish story. Maybe a stubborn Passover allegory found its way across time to the tables at Oslo.

Empathy for the pain of others is meant to be a Jewish value, and it is even a condition that brings comfort to Jews from others—when we let them in.

I remember when a friend called me in the hours following the report that Israel's prime minister, Yitzhak Rabin, had died of his gunshot wounds. My friend does not share my religion, heritage, or racial background. My friend is a Baptist minister. But we obviously share something that transcends any of the differences—our humanity, especially in times that sometimes feel so inhuman. My friend expressed his sadness about the killing, and his condolences for what happened "to your people, to all of us."

Indeed, the collective grief of people in the Jewish community over that horrific act will be deep and lasting. Any of us with personal connections to Israel found it particularly devastating to have to integrate the notion of an Israeli citizen walking up to the democratically elected prime minister and shooting him dead. It betrayed every instinct that was instilled in my generation during those early days of the Jewish state.

But some other things instilled in us back then were somewhat undone by that tragedy of November 1995. These things were not necessarily noble or helpful; listening to Passover, we might discover and understand this. In the unraveling of these prior ideas there is some bittersweet redemption, even a wisp of hope.

At the top of this emotional rewrite was our fundamental belief, through most of the years since Israel was created in 1948, that somebody from outside our national family would never weep with us at a time like that. An irony: The people whose rabbis wrote the Passover tale about empathy were not expecting any empathy from anybody else.

At the time of the funeral of Yitzhak Rabin, however, things changed. The obvious sorrow of President Bill Clinton (whose sympathetic pronouncement in Hebrew of *"shalom, chaver"* wound up reprinted on countless Israeli bumper stickers), the evident bereavement of Jordan's King Hussein, and the apparent shock of PLO Chairman Yasser Arafat added up to a new equation for the Jewish people in general and for the nation of Israel specifically.

On one level, the reactions of these men, their public involvement in the grieving process, indicated that Yitzhak Rabin was a transcendent figure who inspired many people from many categories. Even his former adversaries, enemies of Israel, had come to love and admire him.

The personal impact on public men of this martyr created the new reality that Christians and Muslims joined Jews in shedding the salty waters of their grief together on a hillside in Jerusalem. It was an uncanny display of pure empathy across national lines. Former strangers had become intimate with each other's ideals, visions, and frustrations. They became, on various levels, kindred spirits. Perhaps what they had come to share the most was their unyielding, equalizing mortality. *"My children are perishing . . ."*

When my generation was young children in the relatively new Israel, we experienced a certain insulation that both comforted us and isolated us. The Arabs were real and dangerous enemies; some remain so to this day. Certainly, their public figures embodied our worst fears and biases. I clearly recall, while living in the border village of Kfar Saba, adjacent to the hostile Jordanian hamlet of Qalqilya, that we children actually referred to King Hussein as "Haman"—the historical and genocidal villain of the Purim story.

Yasser Arafat of the PLO emerged much later. His vilification by Israeli children and adults for all the years until

the Oslo breakthrough was understandable and necessary. Too often it was the direct result of grief felt by surviving members of a family victimized by PLO–directed
or –inspired violence, from Munich to Athens to Entebbe
to Tel Aviv. We had reasons to reflect on the leaders of
the PLO during our Passover seders among the tormen-
tors of our people.

Meanwhile, in Israel we always celebrated the historic
friendship of the United States, but we nevertheless felt
uncertain that American leaders truly felt our pain, our
yearnings, our predicament. I think that we developed
our own bias that the leader of America could not ultimately relate to the Holocaust–affected but resilient story
of the Jewish state.

But after Yitzhak Rabin was struck down, there came
President Clinton to Mount Herzl, with his tears, his
woe, his crooked yarmulke riding precariously but sincerely upon his Christian head. A host of Americans were
there, mingling with sheiks, princes, kings, and ministers
from around the world that most Jews had instinctively
believed didn't care for us or about us. The president of
Egypt and the king of Jordan—at considerable peril to
themselves—prayed for their "brother and friend."

Of course, not everybody in the Arab world shared the
instincts of those who came to grieve with the Jewish
people that day. Not everyone in the world would have
heeded the rabbinic message of the Passover parable
about the ministering angels who forgot to see the big
picture. But in the story, in its moral code, is the plea that

we not fail to humanize even those whom we oppose. On a Jerusalem hillside not long ago, it seemed that a lot of us, Jew, Christian, and Muslim, were able to discover that, in the end, tears, like bullets or sea waves, do not know any particular religion.

Ever since that first Passover, it is very unlikely that any angels in heaven have rejoiced when somebody died while somebody else lived—from the Sea of Reeds to San Salvador to Sarajevo.

## Chapter Ten

# We Are All Egyptians, We Are All Hebrews

A story emerged in the Middle East nearly twenty years ago about a young Israeli boy and his mother. When the great news came that the president of Egypt, Anwar el-Sadat, had arrived in Jerusalem to make peace, the mother began weeping with joy, relief, and hope. "My son will not have to die fighting Egyptians," she said in between sobs. Her son, seven or eight years old at the time, clung to his mother. He looked up at her and asked her a question: "Mommy, do you think that right now a mother in Egypt is holding onto her son like you are and is also crying with happiness?"

"Yes, I'm sure of that, my child," came the answer. "That's what peace is all about."

As we have learned from the Jewish tradition, God created us one by one in order to teach us that no one is superior to the other. But there is an ongoing verisimilitude about the alikeness of people that goes beyond the creation equation. The Passover story, through the examples of its two key antagonists, illustrates that people are more or less the same potential amalgam of good and bad qualities. In many ways, we are all Egyptians, we are all Hebrews.

It would be easy to assume, from a superficial reading of the Passover account, that Moses was pretty much all good and that Pharaoh was simply a villain. We tend to color things in black and white. This bias may apply well to the clear-cut, intellectual struggle between freedom and slavery, but as it characterizes people, the practice falls victim to the reality of the gray.

Before examining the subtleties of Pharaoh and Moses, it is worth noting the manner in which the Bible generally presents its characters. The fact is that the Hebrew scriptures, from start to finish, are not embellished with too many models of perfection. Adam and Eve are failures at divine gardening; their son Cain murders his own brother. Noah may have been "a righteous man in his times," as Genesis suggests. But what kind of times were these? These were times so rotten that "the earth was corrupt before God . . . filled with violence." The human race was so contemptible in those times that God decided to end it. Not such great times, after all. Against such a backdrop Noah's character may not have been so terrific. He was just the best of a bad lot. Meanwhile, the rabbis have little patience for Noah's inability even to question God when God announces the end of humankind. It's safe to say that Noah's most assertive inquiry during the discourse is: "So how many cubits should the ark be?"

Abraham and Sarah betray some sullen qualities during their long and sometimes restive marriage. At key moments Abraham is noticeably insensitive to his wife's physical and emotional needs. Isaac is simpleminded and aloof regarding the tension between his twin sons. Their mother, Rebekah, is unabashedly duplicitous in arranging some knavery that pulls the birthright from Esau to Jacob. As a father, Jacob openly favors Joseph among his twelve sons, leading to attempted fratricide, family dysfunction, and a permanent estrangement among the unhappy brothers. None of these patriarchs has a particularly lofty view of women, be they wives or concubines.

Aaron, the brother of Moses, is indecisive and sometimes hapless. He and his sister, Miriam, are clearly resentful of their celebrated brother from time to time. In later scriptural epochs we find the melancholia of Saul, the nymphomania of David, the vanity of Solomon, and arbitrariness and even cruelty of a host of kings and seers. In short, these are real men and women who occupy and motivate these great and edifying stories of human yearnings, and occasional heavenly interventions. They are sometimes heroic, frequently small-minded, always human. They have an enduring power in theological literature because they are—like us—diverse, complicated, moody, and mortal. None of their dramas preclude the notion that people on both sides of a conflict can be petty, decent, mirthful, vengeful, or have the capacity to cry with their children. To one degree or another, we are all Philistines, we are all Canaanites, Jebusites, Judeans, Egyptians, Babylonians.

It is already clear, from Chapter 6, that Moses was decidedly mortal. He is not vaulted by the Passover story into a state of impeccability. That is good because, among other things, Moses was a murderer.

One needs to recall the dramatic biblical story about Moses and his outrage when he witnesses the particular brutality of a nameless Egyptian taskmaster. Moses was still living as an Egyptian prince at the time, but had apparently begun to identify with his birth people, the Hebrews. Exodus tells us that *"when Moses was grown, he went out to his brethren and looked on their burden."* On a walk one day he is unable to tolerate the way in which a whip is being applied to a faltering Hebrew slave. In a moment of uncontrollable vehemence, perhaps mixed with confusion and guilt, Moses slays the Egyptian supervisor. This, of course, abruptly ends Moses' comfortable stay in Egypt; he immediately becomes a fugitive from Pharaoh's judicial system.

The rabbinic tradition is preoccupied and troubled by this cathartic event that catapulted Moses to the quiet fields of Midian and his eventual return to Egypt as the world's first civil rights leader. The fact is that Moses has blood on his hands, even if his motives were noble and inspired. No amount of rationalization can do away with the overriding reality of what Moses did; as one Jewish commentator has put it, "it surely savored of unlawful vengeance and anger."

There are, of course, a variety of opinions about this incident, including the notion that Moses had no choice, and that, even though murder violates every decent civilized code, he was in a predicament that compelled him to take the law into his own hands. None of these explications is very satisfying, particularly the assertion drawn from the work of the famed commentator Maimonides that the killing was justified under the law of the "pursuer." This rabbinic safety valve advances the controversial view that a Jew is permitted, even obliged, to kill when he is rescuing the victim from the pursuer. Moses was rescuing a victim from his Egyptian "pursuer"—the heartless taskmaster who smote the slave.

It might be noted that this exact same polemic was used by some right-wing religious fanatics to justify the murder of Israeli prime minister Yitzhak Rabin in 1995. At the time, some rabbis in Israel referred to this same decree of "the pursuer"—citing the martyred Rabin as a "pursuer" of the Jewish people who was endangering Israel by exchanging holy land for peace agreements with the Arabs. Therefore, the assassin was actually doing the right thing in behalf of "the victim"—the Jewish people. The vast majority of the Jewish world condemned this line of thinking as a reprehensible corruption of religious law.

The comparison of the Rabin case and the biblical incident is made only for purposes of discussion. Most people who in any way rationalize what Moses did to an Egyptian thug nevertheless find the assassin of Yitzhak Rabin a totally despicable person. The fact remains, however, that Moses committed a murder that requires quite a bit of soul-searching in Jewish tradition. This is as it should be; no one of any culture is wholly without impurities. Generally speaking, Jewish literature is honest about the flaws of even the most exalted of our heroes. King David, for example, is prohibited from building the Holy Temple in Jerusalem because he had been a warrior for too long and simply had too much blood on his hands.

We may conclude that Moses was not all good, and that he certainly shared in the prevailing human admixture of virtue and vice. Can a case be made that his adversary, Pharaoh, was not an altogether bad person? A feeble case perhaps, in light of the slavery of millions that Pharaoh promulgated. Again, Passover makes no compromises on the issue of human dignity. Pharaoh was surely not a nice person, or enlightened, or in any way worth emulating. But the Passover story itself does give us some grounds for wondering if he really was as completely a benighted individual as we might assume.

We infer, naturally, that Pharaoh was obdurate on the question of freedom for his Hebrew slaves. The basic premise of the Passover story is founded on the tension between the pleading Moses and the unrelenting Egyptian king. Over and over Moses demands: *"Let my people go!"* To each entreaty Pharaoh is shown to be implacable and heartless. Indeed, it is his heart that provides the image of intractability. In the text, Pharaoh's heart "hardens" with each visit from Moses and Aaron, and after each of the first nine plagues.

But is Pharaoh really permitted to be himself during the course of this dynamic? A look at Exodus, chapter seven, might make us a little uneasy about the whole thing. God tells Moses: *"And I will harden Pharaoh's heart, and multiply my signs and my wonders in the land of Egypt."*

You really can't be altogether sure about where Pharaoh's stubbornness is coming from in this story. Granted, you can be certain that he is a fairly selfish and egotistical individual, with little tolerance for humanity. There is no evidence in the Scripture that this king, unlike a host of other non-Hebrew characters, has a capacity for tenderness and amiability. But the fact remains that, repeatedly, it is God who successively and systematically hardens Pharaoh's heart, allowing for the continuation of the great, public disputation between the two contending sides. If the king had opted for an early resolution of the crisis—if perhaps he possessed the innate capacity to sympathize with the slaves—God was not taking any chances. This leaves us with two considerations: Pharaoh, though clearly an untoward fellow, may not have been as malevolent as we assume. Moreover, God may have wanted to exacerbate Pharaoh's royal willfulness in order to play out this drama for the benefit of posterity.

The biblical text leaves no doubt that heaven played a role in Pharaoh's disposition as the story unfolded. The text is very specific about the source of "hardening" following the sixth through ninth plagues. After the plague of boils (six), we read the announcement: *"Then the Lord hardened the heart of Pharaoh so that he would not listen to them, as the Lord had spoken to Moses."* Similar descriptions follow each subsequent plague; the king never had a chance to soften his personality! Even the great Jewish sage Nachmanides wonders: What was Pharaoh's crime, after all? God was pulling all of the coronary strings and essentially denying the king a full measure of free will.

As in the case of Moses' capital crime, the rabbinic tradition has no firm conclusion about the true predilection of Pharaoh's heart. Some of the arguments suggest that the divine hardening reflected only the king's real bias, anyway. Other explanations stress that in order for the lesson of the confrontation to be borne out—namely, that slavery is wrong and freedom is right—God had to extract a full measure of cooperative intransigence from a pernicious monarch whose ultimate immorality was already etched in the very nature of his kingdom. This demonstration of heaven's intent to prove the merit of benevolence required a ten-fold measure of divine histrionics in order to be enlightening and binding for all time.

But the question remains: Just how bad was this bad king? Left to his own wits, might he have shown a better temperament before ten plagues and a full national humiliation were thrust upon him and his people? I don't think we really know everything about Pharaoh's character, although we assuredly know that he would not have been a candidate for the Nobel peace prize. A certain hedge against unrestrained judgmentalism might be in order when we consider that the good Moses killed somebody and that the bad Pharaoh never really had his own heart.

The Passover story, grounded in the pursuit of tolerance, begs us to be tolerant. It is so easy for any of us, especially in a cultural mosaic like America, to assume character traits about other individuals and groups. I don't really plead a case here for Pharaoh; I only suggest that his story calls us to examine other people's hearts carefully before rushing to judgment. Nor, as has already been asserted in this book, does the Passover story offer us a double standard for morality regarding the Jewish nation and others.

So often, sitting around the Seder table, we are moved by the wonderful, reassuring conception of God "hearing the cries of the Hebrews." We feel special, comforted by the notion that where people are enslaved, heaven will eventually hearken and intervene. Whether the intervention actually emanates from the firmament or from the moral indignation of people on earth who are sufficiently motivated, the biblical implications are the same: The anguish of the Hebrews aroused a new spiritual standard. In response to the cries of the persecuted Hebrews, the intolerant Egyptians were punished and defeated.

But the Bible applies the same standard to the Jewish people soon enough. It's not long after the departure from Egypt—just at a time when the Hebrews might have wallowed in their status—that God turns the ethical tables back upon them—and all of us. *"And a stranger shalt thou not wrong, neither shalt thou oppress him; for ye were strangers in the land of Egypt."*

Indeed, the Bible even turns the same linguistic device on the free Hebrews that was used in their behalf when they were the oppressed ones. God warns them, now that they have control of their own destiny, that they are not to betray the same intolerance for others that the Egyptians showed them. If they afflict others—the widows, the orphans, the disenfranchised, and the disadvantaged— heaven will have ears for these souls just as it did for the enslaved Hebrews: *"If thou afflict them in any wise, for if they cry at all unto me, I will surely hear their cry."*

Nobody in the world, Passover is telling us, has a premium on the human heart—be it hard or soft. Nor is the human heart organically different, whether it beats in the mother thanking God for peace or in a king trying to come to grips with reality. Hearts start out the same; the difference comes with time, circumstance, and how much tolerance is pumped along with the blood.

## Chapter Eleven

# Elijah Rides His Chariot Through the Mall

At Passover there are eight days (seven in Israel and in liberal Jewish circles), four cups, four questions, ten plagues, and, quite often, many people at the table. But there is only one Cup of Elijah—regardless of how opulent or simple the surroundings. The Jewish people, generally skeptical of messianism, usually circumspect about miracles, certainly jaded by history, nevertheless share in the universal practice of setting aside the singular cup for an elusive, mythical, and mysterious figure no one can see but everyone honors.

My brother Sam used to enjoy donning a white sheet and reentering the dining room as the intrepid Elijah just as we were chanting the prophet's song, *Eliahu ha-navi*— "Elijah the Prophet." The young kids present would be delighted and slightly unnerved; all eyes were on the ceremonial cup, whose contents somehow evaporated just a little. Meanwhile, we all would sing in Hebrew:

> *Elijah, the prophet, Elijah the Tishbite,*
> *Elijah, Elijah, Elijah from the region of Gilead.*
> *Quickly will he come to us in our days,*
> *With the messianic son of David.*

The biblical source for this melodramatic moment in the evening is found in the Book of Malachi: *"Behold, I will send you Elijah the prophet, and he will turn the hearts of the parents to the children and the hearts of the children to the parents before the coming of the great and awesome Day of the Lord!"*

Interesting that the moment of messianic redemption, recorded in Scripture, recited every Passover, is envisioned as the reconciliation between children and parents. A simple and sweet eschatology, indeed. Family peace is at the heart of world peace, according to the biblical dreams of the Jewish people. No poetry here of gods, worlds, tremors, culminating struggles; no lyrics pertaining to the End of Days. When Elijah comes, with his friendship for humanity, his consolation for everyone's suffering, he will have come because parents and children started to truly listen to each other. The ultimate hopes of humankind can be realized at home, perhaps around the Seder table.

Elie Wiesel has written that "we have no better defender in heaven than Elijah." Wiesel describes the Tishbite seer as the ultimate witness, "the chronicler, the historian, of Jewish distress. . . . He is the memory of the Jewish people." It's all part of the layered belief of our people, just as the actual practice of "letting Elijah in" has a number of explanations. But a straight reading of

Malachi's declaration places the responsibility for saving the world squarely on the collective members of human families. I have always considered it crucial that—in the very way we Jews celebrate the Passover holiday—we elaborate on the reality that for a miracle to happen, one of us has to open a door somewhere. And that door is invariably right at home.

Meanwhile, why have we been performing this strange ritual for so many centuries? Before turning to its meaning in today's world of the mall culture, it might be important to consider the strange, even painful reasons for the old ritual of leaving a special cup for an invisible visitor to enter and consume. Like so many things Jewish, the origins of this custom have as much to do with practicalities as with piety.

I have mentioned previously that the Jews were accused, most notably in the Middle Ages, of the blood libel. This has been an intermittent fact of life for Jews across many centuries; the problem surfaced in a remote corner of Kentucky only recently. The scandalous charge has been that as Passover approached, Jewish people murdered Christians, especially Christian youth, to gain access to their blood. The Jews would then use the drained blood, according to this slander, to help in the baking of matzoh. The blood would also be drunk ritualistically as though it were the wine of the holiday.

This is an unimaginable defamation, this blood accusation. But so has history often been proven to be unimaginable. Nevertheless, as the encyclopedist Nathan

Ausubel reports: "There was hardly a time or a country in Christian Europe in which Jews did not stand mortally in fear of their lives on account of the frequency of this accusation, which erupted more than once in massacres." The calumny, incidentally, did not just originate in the streets of so many towns and villages. It came, often enough, directly from the pulpits of churches. Priests joined rabble-rousers in stirring the masses against Jewish families who were just trying to observe and celebrate the Seder. This is where the Cup of Elijah, and its attendant rite, came into usefulness for the sometimes desperate Jewish community.

The practice of opening the door for Elijah developed as a way to literally allow suspicious or murderous Christian neighbors *a chance to see that nobody was drinking blood around the Seder table*. In fact, so tragic and uncertain was this situation that for many centuries, the rabbis actually banned the use of red wine for the Four Cups at the Seder. Red wine invited perilous speculation. To safeguard parents and children in their homes, white or raisin wine was frequently substituted.

So what about here and now, when we can drink any flavor of wine we wish, when we are blessed not only with a full array of choices in every category, but with the nearly automatic inclusion of Passover in the substance of American media and advertising? What about now, when we participate in the growing trend toward interfaith and community seders, when Christian neighbors are welcomed into our springtime rituals and we into theirs? We note from recent history that the illustrious Rabbi Kook of Palestine used to invite the British military governor to the rabbi's seder at home—just to keep things open and clear. What about now, when the arrival of Good Friday does not strike dread into our hearts, with the expectation of a routine pogrom? What about now, when Easter and Passover are juxtaposed commercially, not unlike, although not to the same degree, as Christmas and Chanukah? What about now, when we open the door for Elijah, expecting not an invasion of bloodthirsty evil-doers, but the impending completion of a sometimes lengthy evening?

I think that the role of the ethereal Elijah in opulent times such as now has a lot to do with the human imagination. Surely, the rite of Elijah's cup is about hope, and it is assuredly about our continual yearning for a better world. It certainly is a moment that gives wings to our dreams for a peaceful planet. But even as Passover metamorphosed over the centuries to accommodate us when and where we lived, so does it speak to us in today's culture about the need for us to imagine and be curious. The moment of Elijah's cup is the implement for this transformation.

Everybody is in a big hurry these days. Everybody gets what he or she needs or wants quickly, efficiently, dispassionately. We don't just live in homes, we dwell in something called cyberspace. We don't often write letters on paper, using ink or lead. Something gracious and intimate is thereby lost. Nowadays we often transmit messages on a web; we exchange notions across an electronic network where there are nebulous coordinates referred to as "rooms." We don't have genuine conversations too often; we interface. We don't really live in a world of ideas; we participate in a global network of video, fiber optics, and digital instruments. When we think of something we desire, we frequently "call it up" on some keyboard. We don't *imagine* it very often.

We shop in controlled spaces maintained by computer-monitored air ducts and music units. The village square of our European great-grandparents or the main street of our American grandparents or even the open-air shopping center of our parents is replaced by the streamlined portals of the mall civilization. The service is good, the discourse is poor. The malls themselves are already threatened by the proliferating culture of home shopping networks that allow us access, via secret codes and plastic cards, to examine, reject, or order whatever we choose, from automobiles to exercise machines to postgraduate degrees. Not much is conjured up; it's programmed, recalled, erased, or reinstituted. We withdraw money, make payments, order meals, and pump gasoline by punching in numbers and by not ever having a conversation with anybody about anything at any time. I may be sentimental, but I miss the days when a service station attendant I personally met in some exotic state far from home actually walked up to my car window and asked, with genuine interest: "Where are you folks from?"

Elijah calls me back to my imagination. His cup is a

goblet of dreaming, a last, tiny bastion of curiosity. All I have to deal with his bittersweet "appearance" are my wits. Thank God! I depend on his annual visit, on the delicious mystery of his evaporating potion, to reinstate my intuition, my imaginativeness, my sense of personal responsibility for what is conveyed in between human souls. I breathe in the vapors of that noble cup as if for the fickle evidence of human creativity. In a world of programmed sensibilities, Elijah comes to restore my fancy. As against the superimposition of MTV, and the full host of twenty-four-hour, all-color, remote-operated, universally compatible, stereophonic, coaxial, cable-ready, cellular, audio, and visual accouterment of daily life, the sublime prophet whisks his way into the life of a room, a synagogue, a catering hall, a collection of minds, calling back human reverie. It's hard to think of something more redeeming for young people today, who get most of their information and whatever is left of their inspiration from video packages.

Are we too jaded as a society to believe in such an idea? The pervasive loneliness out there, the growth of cults, the proliferation of social groups espousing self-esteem, power, recognition, or just some kind of "connection," tell me otherwise. Our civilization is full of information, bereft of knowledge. We *need* to imagine some things; we *need* to receive some input from something other than a computer terminal. We need to dream; that's all that Elijah, the slippery seer, calls us to do during a special night of watching, reflecting, and rediscovering.

We need the enlightenment of having to speculate and make a decision from within ourselves.

Biblical lore tells us that Elijah never actually dies. In the second Book of Kings, he is busy with his disciple Elisha when he is suddenly whisked heavenward in a fiery chariot. Unlike most biblical heroes, Elijah constantly reappears—at seders and also at ceremonies of circumcision. In the course of his earthly career he ostensibly performs miracles, involving food and reviving the dead, that are clearly literary models for the attributed activities of Jesus of Nazareth several centuries later.

What would happen if Elijah came through the mall today on board his blazing chariot? Such a cataclysm would undoubtedly be covered live on CNN, and later rerun and analyzed on successive tabloid news magazines. The prophet's private life would likely be turned over for possible scandals. But maybe, just maybe, his wild ride through our very formatted lives would light a fire in the chariot of our souls.

The idea of Elijah is a good thing for us in the 1990s. How often do we just open the door, dream a little, and surreptitiously check to see if a magical cup needs replenishing or not? How often do we just wonder if there's something out there that is more than what we can plainly see?

## Chapter Twelve

# Cleaning the House, Cleaning the Soul

It's really not that long after Purim, usually sometime in March, when the coming of Passover begins to be felt along the shelves, in the kitchen cabinets, about the refrigerator, and certainly in the bread box. A transformation occurs that is consonant with the secular habit of the so-called "spring cleaning." Granted, in some homes the pre-Passover cleansing is more intense, more stylized, than in others. Not every Jew is obsessed with carrying out the religiously explicit *bedikat hametz*—the "search for leaven." But generally speaking, there is an air of refreshing inquiry, of invigorating emergence, as the winter gives way to the reawakening of spring.

As far away as China, Jews have linked Passover to the spring cycle of their particular culture. Who anywhere would not open the windows, lean into the warmer breeze, smell the new blossoms, gaze upon the reborn green buds, notice the returning birds, and then not be buoyed by fresh hope? Who would not sense the new season and savor the rush of freedom?

The Jews of Kaifeng joined Passover to the Chinese springtime rite of renewal. Passover, uniquely suited to observance in one's own house, was entirely anticipated and celebrated at home; there had been no synagogue in China, according to the scholar Xu Xin, since the middle of the nineteenth century.

Indeed, the Chinese Jews mimicked the biblical, paschal story by using the blood of either a lamb or a rooster, or just some red paint, to smear across their door posts. This, of course, was a symbolic rendering of what their Hebrew ancestors in Egypt did on the Night of Watching, directing the Angel of Death to *pass over* their homes. Then they sat down to their Seder feasts, using a flat, Chinese unleavened bread called *luobin*. They also tasted a harsh soup, made from mutton, that, like our horseradish, reminded the participants of the bitterness of slavery.

While their neighbors often erected Buddhist icons in their homes during the Chinese springtime festival, the Jews of China, like Jews from Australia to Russia, have worshiped the idea of freedom every spring. From Kaifeng to Kansas, from Cleveland to Cairo, Jewish households have busied themselves with some form of internal inspection and cleansing in the fragrant days before Passover. It's good for the habitation, good for the soul.

It might be worthwhile to examine what the most stringent Jews are doing during this rite of domestic ablution. Since the Bible prohibits the consumption of *hametz* (leaven) during the days of Passover, there is a Talmudic mandate for the search and removal of any traces of leaven in the period just before the festival. According to Isaac Klein's *A Guide to Jewish Religious Practice*, leaven refers to food derived from several kinds of grain, including wheat, barley, oats, spelt, and rye. Some rabbis have also added rice, millet, corn, and legumes to the list. As with most things Jewish, there is creative disagreement on the extent of the restrictions; the spiritual charge to cleanse one's surroundings as the seasons change transcends the discussion.

The matzoh, of course, is usually made from wheat flour that has obviously not been allowed to leaven. All traces of leaven, or of food containing leavened components, must be removed from the premises. You can wipe it away, you can even burn it. But it has to be gone before the holiday arrives.

For the devout, there is a solemn procedure. Pronouncing special benedictions, the house is searched by the light of a candle. Any renegade crumbs are swept away with a special feather. In fact, since the house has undoubtedly already been cleaned by the time of these waning hours before the holiday, a few bread crumbs are deliberately left in conspicuous spaces. They are "found" and the correct blessings are said in order to fulfill the ritual with a sense of satisfaction. There are even rules and special prayers that involve the final burning of leaven crumbs on the morning prior to the first Seder, as well as provisions for temporarily "selling" the excess leaven to a cooperative gentile neighbor. There are detailed procedures to follow if you happen to be traveling during the thirty days just before the holiday is set to begin.

What does it all mean in the category of the soul?

I think that all of these rites, to whatever extent observed or experienced, add up to a kind of Talmudic equivalent of "getting in touch with yourself." When you look for leaven, you just might find some other things that remind you who you are. You may discover who it is that you love or have neglected to love. An examination of a kitchen drawer can draw out memories. Since we are prone, in this era of fast, packaged food, to snack in almost every room at home, the emotional "search party" ought to be extended throughout the house. A quest, on my part, into the little drawer at my bedpost a few years ago yielded me not only a discarded candy wrapper but also a war medal given to my late father by the Israel Defense Forces in 1949. As a result my father, who long ago conducted the Seder in my childhood home, made a special visit to the ceremony that I subsequently led with my children.

Beyond the liable crumbs, there are memorable theater tickets, keys to forgotten doors, lapsed certificates, misplaced report cards, lumpy baseballs, flattened candles, widowed gloves, crumpled letters, wrinkled photographs, and unlikely political buttons. Rediscovered, such things create important associations. Ten years after working tirelessly for the campaign, my wife, Cathy, and I found a stubborn lapel pin marked MONDALE/FERRARO. Wiping the drawer clean for Passover, we thought about how our country has changed since the old pin was thrown in with an assortment of screwdrivers, AC adapters, bottle caps, an extension cord, and a few depreciated dreams.

The springtime turnover in anticipation of Passover also includes the very utensils and dishware used during the festival. Many families have dishes designated exclusively for the holiday. If that is not practical, regular dishes may be employed, but only if the utensils undergo an extensive washing process that supposedly purges them of any residual leaven. Dishes, like foods, can be made "kosher" under the correct rabbinical guidelines. In any case, the pulling or reassigning of plates, glasses, cups, knives, spoons, and forks also inspire an examination of what one owns, how one eats, with whom one eats.

Going through the nooks and crannies of a house while newly opened windows deliver the scent of fresh blossoms, we detect fingerprints from the past. Preparing for a timely reunion with family and friends at the imminent Seder, we make ready with the grasping of old trinkets, poignant notes, jolting photos, precious diaries. We revisit histories; we may even rearrange the emotional agenda for the coming holiday gathering. Turning to the kitchen cabinets, where the thrust of the leaven search is directed, we may find the memory tickled, a fondness reawakened by the sight of a forgotten but venerable glass container of homemade jam, or an old jar of pickles, or a little box of a certain spice. Open drawers reveal open souls.

It should be noted that the revelation of worthy values that comes with the spring "search" can and should be extended to beyond the walls of one's residence. Peering through well-stocked cabinets reminds us that many others in America are hungry. Their shelves and their stomachs are horribly depleted; an intolerable number of people subsisting in our cities lack even the shelves. While the traditional custom of burning a few bread crumbs may have a redeeming ritualistic value, bread should not be burned away in this very unequal society. Looking into your own stock, take stock of society's terrible inequities. Canned goods that do not qualify as Passover foods, inappropriate loaves, grains, cereals, cookies, or crackers should not simply be removed or retired from sight. Give them to the hungry, thus making the level of your observance of Passover spiritually honest. Quibble less about what is "glatt" (stringently) kosher in your home and more about what is "glatt" hunger in your country.

The spring housecleaning is only as purifying as the moral cleansing it offers. Like most of the rites of Passover, the exploration of one's environment helps make us feel responsible for one another. The things we do at Passover are redemptive *because we actually do them.* This reality is as old as the Book of Exodus and as new as your own family journal. As I have suggested throughout this book, Passover is not directed from heaven as much as it is experienced directly in your own world. This challenge is borne out in Elie Wiesel's cogent observation: "Man has conquered space, but not his own heart."

The holiday anthologist Philip Goodman has written: "Perhaps more than any other Jewish holiday, Passover requires considerable expenditures of time, energy, and material resources." Yes, it takes a measure of commitment, planning, caring, and thoughtfulness to prepare a house, search for leaven, acquire a panoply of special foods, rearrange a kitchen, serve an elaborate and religiously sanctioned meal involving an array of staged and timed passages and requirements. You don't go to the rabbi for this one; the spiritual value is neither delivered nor transmitted. You yourself, rubbing shoulders physically and numinously with people from your past and present, make it happen. The theology of Passover is as much in your hands as it is in any holy book.

Passover, arriving on the wings of spring, is the charter Jewish holiday. It exists without the synagogue; in fact, it first happened not in the ancient Holy Temple of Jerusalem, but outdoors, amidst the vineyards, wheat stalks, and date trees of the Canaanite countryside. Cleansing themselves as a free nation, the first festival shared by the Hebrews after entering the Holy Land was Passover. The account is found in the Book of Joshua.

Interesting that these were not the original slaves who had escaped from Egypt. With the exception of Joshua himself, and his acolyte Caleb, these Passover celebrants were *the children* of the liberated Egyptian slaves. The forty years of wandering in the desert had allowed the generation of bondsmen to die out; their offspring, who had been born free, were the ones able to inherit the land and the tradition. These descendants, who had not been despoiled by bondage, were more likely to appreciate what they actually possessed. Perhaps a similar lesson is in store for us, living in imperially affluent times, as we sift through our drawers and cabinets and closets, searching for elusive crumbs and for new meanings.

With the transformation in the new land, with the first national Seder, came a religious calendar, a call for community, an understanding that people live and die in the cycle of generations. Being a parent invokes responsibility; being a child endows a family story. Passover was the first spring cleaning of the world house. Passover gave us command of history, after heaven had opened the door. Now, however, we no longer wait for plagues to deliver us; we must devise and create the remedies that will save us. On the wisp of a sweet springtime breeze, Passover calls us to clean our homes and to cleanse our souls.

I am intrigued by the old custom of lighting a candle, taking one another by the hand, and searching the house for those bits and pieces of impurity that may linger in a house that was sealed up for too long. Even for those who are not so devout, it may be a useful exercise. You may indeed find a guilty scrap. You may find some insight as well. Clasping someone with one hand, and a simple candle in the other, the flickering wick may reveal someone you love in a soft, new light.

༄༅

# "For Your Love Is
# Better Than Wine . . ."

In the beginning, there was love. Before the beginning, there was nothingness. God grew lonely and longed for partners. So in the beginning, driven by love, God created a garden. In it God placed a man and a woman. Their relationship was love. The man and the woman looked to each other in the same way as did the heaven and the earth. In the beginning, it was love that filled the oceans, embraced the countrysides, fueled the starshine.

Then love was bent, because people are flawed. There was bloodshed, slavery, humiliation, and eventually a great flood. The last drop of water was a tear from the eyes of God. Love had been deflected through the jagged prism of human nature.

There was renewal, and God's promise not to destroy again. Perhaps God knew that people would be destructive enough by themselves. It was clear that the refraction of good and evil was a constant of the human soul. Civilization spread all through the earth, sometimes planting gardens, sometimes scorching the ground. There was smoke in the sky, slavery in the nations, barriers and walls where once heaven had planted gardens.

There were also moments of tenderness, such as when an Egyptian princess found and saved a doomed Hebrew baby among the bulrushes. The child, Moses, grew and discovered his love for his own, forsaken people. Later, as a fugitive in the hills of Midian, he gave his heart in love to a woman of the shepherds. He eventually returned to the land of the bulrushes to remind a stubborn king that human beings are diminished when we do not love one another. When the king finally agreed to let the people go, the heavenly angels certainly sighed with nostalgia. In so many human hearts the original garden was being replanted. Or so the angels believed.

Moses of the bulrushes had been reluctant to face the king. Something had compelled him, however. Some say it was a bush he encountered one day in the hills. One of his flock had wandered off, and the shepherd came across a bush that burned but was not consumed. God spoke to Moses through the bush. Others say, however, that Moses just knew inside to go back and protest against the slavery of his countrymen. Something made him believe that bondage was wrong and that freedom was right.

If not directly God and the bush, what could have made Moses feel this way? Some say it was love, and I agree. In those quiet hills of Midian, Moses felt love—for the cycle of the sun and the moon, for the breakthrough of morning, for the stillness of night. Moses also knew love for his wife, Zipporah. He was a man who had seen slavery but now lived with a heart as free as the wind, as contented as the warm presence of his beloved. Love taught Moses how good it is to be free. The burning bush that could not be consumed? That could have very well been God's rendering of the soul of Moses.

So the Hebrews went out from Egypt, and the world had an unforgettable story. The story is valued because its drama, like the Midianite bush, never burns out. People continue to enslave one another. People continue not to get enough love. Pharaohs roam the earth; Moses and Aaron and Miriam and Joshua and Deborah rise up from time to time, demanding: *"Let my people go!"* Men and women who are properly loved cry out to others who must not have had enough love. Sometimes love wins, and babies are saved from the bulrushes. But sometimes babies die. Sometimes people march to freedom. And sometimes they wallow in sadness.

Perhaps the last hope for the human family is love. Perhaps that is why the holiday of Passover closes every springtime with a poem that is supremely and consummately about love. The dishes of the Seder have been washed and put away for almost a week. The holiday tablecloth has been cleansed of the matzoh crumbs, the wine stains, the soup spills. Elijah's cup is back in its place of honor at the top of the dining room cabinet. The Haggadah books are replaced in the drawer, waiting for next year. Most of the visitors who came and tugged the heartstrings have departed. Tears have dried; the songs have subsided. The extra boxes of matzoh that were over-bought sit unopened in the kitchen cabinet; their lot is to be consumed without sanctifying implications. The holiday is receding; it's time to read out loud in the synagogue about a fierce, passionate, even erotic love.

From time immemorial, the end of Passover has been celebrated with the reading of the biblical Song of Songs. This book, one of the beloved Five Scrolls (also including Ecclesiastes, Esther, Ruth, and Lamentations) is attributed to the hand and mind of King Solomon. He was a man who knew a lot about the lusts of the heart. He invited and maintained lovers from the world over. Like his father, David, he had an insatiable fervor for women. This king, known for his wisdom and vision, who designed and built the Holy Temple to God, was an indomitable romantic who fancied the springtime, craved intimacy, and certainly cultivated God's endowed gift of passion. The expressive, even carnal volume known as Song of Songs is considered by the traditional rabbinate as an allegory of God's love for his "bride," Israel. A great deal of this wondrous book is pretty literal, however, invoking such images as *"your breasts are like a cluster of grapes" "sweet honey drops from your lips" "I rose to open for my beloved" "your navel is like a round goblet."* There are amorous metaphors, such as "apples" and "my couch." There is a remarkable literalism here and an unabashed sexuality—all of which is normally read in the synagogue as Passover comes to a conclusion. As Herbert Bronstein and Albert Friedlander have co-written: "This is a collection of lyric love songs in which love is celebrated for its own sake."

Earlier in this book, reference was made to the heroic Rabbi Leo Baeck, the courageous "teacher of Theresienstadt." Baeck, as we discussed, taught ideas while enduring the concentration camp's kingdom of hell. Fueled by an undying love for poetry and beauty, he wrote about King Solomon's eternal love song while struggling to stay alive in the camp. Bronstein and Friedlander quote Baeck in their introduction to the Song of Songs: "Two poetic works that tell of the love of man and woman have been incorporated in the Bible. One is the Song of Solomon . . . which sings of love as awakening in the young soul and in the young body." (The other such work cited by Baeck was the Book of Ruth.)

Again, there in the death camp the rabbi was thinking about freedom, about learning, about love, as the keepers of human sanity. Meanwhile, the vividness of Solomon's love poems have survived scripturally right along with Pharaoh's stubbornness, Miriam's freedom song at the Sea of Reeds, and with the Ten Commandments themselves. Judaism has never divorced itself from reality, and the reality is that men and women crave and deserve freedom just as much as they do one another:

> *The Song of Songs, which is Solomon's.*
> *Let him kiss me with the kisses of his mouth*
> *For your love is better than wine.*
> *Your ointments have a delicate fragrance,*

*Your name is oil poured out—*
*Therefore do the maidens love you. . . .*
*We will remember your love more than wine;*
*How right it is to love you!*

Is it one person's physical need for the other? Is it God courting the people of Israel? Is it earth romancing heaven? Or is it all of these, riding triumphantly on humankind's better nature, even as the frozen waters of winter are thawed by the warmth and charity of spring? Passover is about the changing of the seasons, after all— when oppression ends, when color is reborn, when hope comes back to us across a gentler breeze. Perhaps it was simply *everything good* that the wistful poet king was fancying a long time ago when he wrote:

*Rise up, my love, my fair one, and come away.*
*For lo, the winter is past,*
*The rains are over and gone.*
*The flowers appear on the earth,*
*The time of singing has come,*
*And the voice of the turtle dove is heard in our land.*

For some, it's heaven's cabalistic journal. For others, it's the private passion between a man and a woman. For others still, it's a carnal dance between spiritual forces that live on earth. For Passover, however, it's the last word, and it means that no one is really free until everyone is free to love.

* * *

It whispers to you first as the winter is receding, and you are reopening the drawers of your household and the chambers of your soul. It beckons to you at the Seder table with the lyrics of your ancestors. It calls to you from the troubled, ancient shores of the Nile, and it has been heard about in our time along the Rhine and the Mississippi and so many other rivers of hate. It awakens you with the symphonies of benevolence that have played— from a single set of Egyptian bulrushes to the learning academies of Babylon to the teaching tents of Africa to the spiritual pagodas of China to the caring sanctuaries of Europe to the underground railroads of so many freedom campaigns. It is relevant for every child of every color ever born of a mother who knew how to give the milk of kindness.

When you hear the voices of your parents; when you hear the music of your heritage; when you hear the singing of springtime birds; when you hear the speech of your lover; when you hear your heart telling you to care; when you hear the bells of freedom; that is when you are hearing the Haggadah. And when you are moved by these melodies, and you begin to repair the world around you, that is when you are truly thinking Passover.

·   A NOTE ON THE TYPE   ·

The typeface used in this book is a version of Weiss (also known as Weiss Antiqua), designed in 1926 by Professor Emil Rudolf Weiss (1875–1943) for the Bauer type foundry in Frankfurt, Germany. Weiss, a distinguished graphic artist, was commissioned by Bauer as part of its aggressive program in the 1920s and '30s to encourage new type designs. (Bauer's efforts during this period were paralleled, though on a smaller scale, by English Monotype's under Stanley Morison.) Weiss worked very slowly, but the care he lavished on his design may account for its continuing popularity because it has some quirks that might have prevented its success. Its "upside-down" S has often been noted, an illusion caused by the equal size of the two curves—in contrast to the S of most typefaces, whose upper curve is somewhat smaller; another peculiarity is a marked widening toward the top of the vertical stroke of lowercase letters like l.